BECOMING MARLIS MANN

GROWING UP UNDER HITLER,
SURVIVING THE WAR, MAKING A LIFE, AND
BECOMING MARLIS MANN

A Memoir by Marlis Fasterding Mann
As Told to My Husband, Tom Skinner

Mission Point Press
2554 Chandler Road
Traverse City, MI 49696
www.MissionPointPress.com

The author credits the work of Burchardt Warnecke in his history of Braunschweig, Germany.

First published by Chandler Lake Books, an imprint of Mission Point Press.

Edited by Susan S. Vaupel.
Picture Editor: Geary Hoffman.
Designed by Kelly Ludwig.

Printed in the United States of America.
ISBN: 978-1-943338-08-5
Library of Congress Control Number: 2016941369

CHANDLER LAKE
BOOKS

Growing Up Under Hitler, Surviving
the War, Making a Life, and

BECOMING
MARLIS MANN

A Memoir by Marlis Fasterding Mann
As Told to My Husband, Tom Skinner

To Sandy and Louise
with best regards and love
from
Marlis Mann

For my beloved sister Inge,
who always led the way

PROLOGUE

THE JOURNEY BEGINS

How, you might ask, did this book come to be?

When as newlyweds David and I arrived in Chicago in the winter of 1958 to settle into our tiny garage apartment in Wilmette while Dave went to work at the R.R. Donnelley Company, it was not long before curious friends began to ask questions about my German roots and what it was like to grow up when Adolf Hitler and his National Socialists ruled Germany. How did I survive the war and what was it like to fly for Condor and Lufthansa in those early years? How did David and I meet?

I answered countless questions and told lots of stories. As time went on I was interviewed for newspaper articles and I talked to school children about my early life. Members of the German adult education class I taught for 7 years showered me with questions. I responded with my memories of past events but never thought of putting these things together in a book.

When we built our home and moved to Leland in 1987 it was the same story: Everyone seemed to be curious about how this German girl had survived the war and made her way to this little fishing village in northern Michigan. Again there were talks to school children and to the local Rotary Club in addition to articles in the local Leelanau Enterprise. The more friends we made, it seems, the more stories I was encouraged to tell. Gradually, in the back of my mind, I began to wonder if I might someday put them all together in a book.

Years passed and when Tom Skinner and I became engaged and I realized that he had written and edited scripts for a number of award-winning documentary films, I asked if he would consider writing the story of my early life. I think he said "yes" in a moment of weakness, and somehow the project was born.

We became engaged on the deck of the M.S. Paul Gauguin in French Polynesia in 2009 and returned to the ship to celebrate our first anniversary in 2010. Tom brought along his computer, and we prepared to begin the project in earnest. Curious about what we were doing, the Captain of the ship, Rajko Zupan, invited us to use his private conference room as a place to write. Tom asked questions, I told stories, and he took notes to be refined at a later point.

When we returned home, the interviewing continued. Tom went to work refining the text through multiple drafts, and we asked our good friend Geary Hoffman if he would scan some of the photos from my collection to help illustrate the story. The first scans were made in 2011 and continued through 2015 and 2016. Geary was amazing. He scanned and re-scanned more than 130 pictures, rescuing and repairing along the way. Still, many bear the marks of amateur photography and early post-war processing. So at the outset I had two special people to thank for helping launch the project, Rajko Zupan and Geary Hoffman, in addition to Tom of course.

My sister Inge was immensely important, helping me to remember events and to get my dates straight. Two minds remembering those long-buried details of a past life were certainly better than one, and both were required throughout the writing process. There were many Trans-Atlantic telephone calls.

As we came close to the end it was clear that we required a professional proof reader and editor. Tom asked his sister, Susan Vaupel, if she would take on the task, and we were delighted when she said "yes." Sue is a former English teacher and professional editor of medical/scientific books and journals. She was Senior Technical Editor for the American Journal of Epidemiology at The Johns Hopkins University and Managing Editor of the Journal of the Institute for Laboratory Animal Research at the

National Academy of Sciences. You can imagine that with this impressive professional background, Sue's consent to take on our project was indeed great news. Her advice and counsel have been invaluable. If you enjoy reading this book, part of the credit certainly goes to Sue.

In early March 2016 we left for a vacation in Costa Rica and a special Caribbean cruise aboard the M.S. Tere Moana, once again captained by our friend Rajko Zupan. Sue had sent us a complete edit of the text, and before the cruise ended we had reviewed her work, page by page and line by line, and sent our final comments back to her through an Internet connection generously provided by Captain Zupan. So, Rajko was there at the beginning and at the end of our project; and we thank him for his friendship, his support, and his encouragement.

When it was time to look for a publisher we sought the advice of the only publisher we knew, Barbara Siepker of the Glen Arbor Press. Barbara immediately suggested we contact Doug Weaver at Mission Point Press in Traverse City. From our very first meeting it was clear that Doug would be our publisher. His services would include that of an experienced designer, Kelly Ludwig, in Kansas City. You will see Kelly's sophisticated design throughout the book, and we thank her for working closely with us to develop the overall "look" of the book. We additionally thank Doug for his advice and counsel throughout the final stages of the project.

I have many friends to whom I am indebted for their contributions. Trudy Underhill translated from Russian two important items from the distant past — evidence of an important chapter in the life of my family. In addition, several other good friends agreed to read the manuscript in draft and offer comments for the jacket. They are writer and award-winning television producer Scott Craig; conductor of the Traverse Symphony Orchestra Kevin Rhodes whom David Mann brought to Traverse City; my good friend; my good friend and fellow Rotarian Dick Grout who, when I was only a schoolgirl, came ashore at Normandy on D-Day to help end the war and make my future possible; and my life-long friend the great jazz bassist Eddie de Haas, whom I first met when Bill Coleman agreed that his band would play at Club Marlis. There is also my good friend, accomplished composer, conductor, and musician David Amram, whom I first met at the Domicile du Jazz in 1953.

Finally, my sincere thanks to my dear husband Tom, who helped me sort out the events and experiences of my early life to create what we hope is a readable account of the life of one very lucky person.

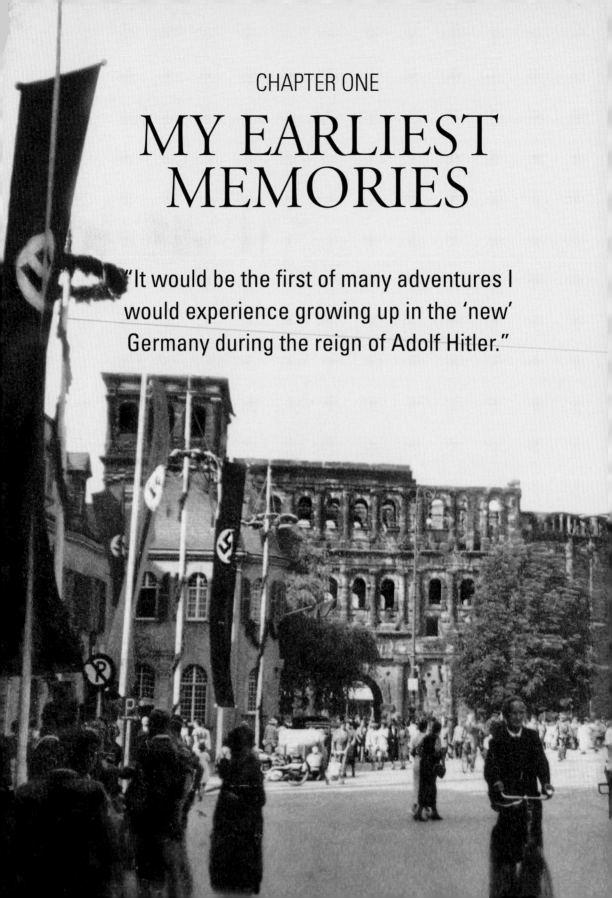

CHAPTER ONE

MY EARLIEST MEMORIES

"It would be the first of many adventures I would experience growing up in the 'new' Germany during the reign of Adolf Hitler."

Nazi banners line the streets in Trier, 1939

Goodbye to the only home I had ever known

My memories begin on February 10, 1937, on the train. For a little girl of three, it was a very long train ride. I only remember being on the train — not why, not where we were going, and certainly not why my sister, my mother, my father, and I needed to leave the only home I had ever known back in Berka, Lower Saxony. It would be the first of many adventures I would experience growing up in the "new" Germany during the reign of Adolf Hitler.

In fact, we were on that train travelling west to join my father. He had gone ahead to find a new job and a new home for us in Trier, the oldest city in Germany founded by the Romans and very near the border with Luxembourg. Years later I would more fully understand the dark reasons why it was necessary for us to move from Berka to Trier.

I remember very little about the trip, although I do recall it was my sister Inge's sixth birthday. She was making the rounds of our fellow passengers announcing the happy event and collecting gifts of candy, which she brought back to share with my mother and me. There were two connections and very long waits between trains. It mattered not at all to Inge or to me that 4 years earlier, in 1933, a little known Austrian named Adolf Hitler had been named Chancellor of Germany and in our lifetime would not only create the most massive war machine the world had ever seen, but would also oversee the murder of millions of innocent people.

In Trier my father, Albert Fasterding, had rented a second floor apartment opposite

An outing with my mother's youngest sister, Lene (far right), and in our new dirndl dresses (below)

the dairy company where he had secured a job as manager, a position for which he had trained in a professional school in Braunschweig. For Inge and for me, life in Trier would be good. I pushed my wooden scooter up and down the sidewalks while Inge went to school. I remember taking boat trips on the Moselle River, and when the weather was warm, Inge and I shared ice cream cones.

One of my playmates was a little girl who lived across the street next to the dairy company. She was my age and she too had a little scooter. She would come to my house often and we would play with our dolls together. Then one afternoon I heard noises in the street in front of our house and ran to the open window. Across the street, in the house where my friend

My big sister and I in Trier

lived, I saw windows being smashed and furniture thrown onto the street. I was scared and screamed for my mother. Down on the street I saw my friend and her parents being loaded onto a truck by German soldiers. When I asked my mother what was going on, I could tell that she was scared too, and I still remember what she said to me: "We can't say or do anything or we'll be on the truck as well." I did not know that my young friend was Jewish nor did I know what it meant to be Jewish in Adolf Hitler's "new" Germany. It would be years later that I would learn the word "Kristallnacht."

My mother had, as I would later say, "played the three monkeys": "Hear nothing, see nothing, speak nothing." She had reason to be fearful, although she could not know how the rise of National Socialism and the Second World War would change our lives forever. But then, I am getting ahead of my story.

In Trier I remember going out to the countryside one beautiful summer day to visit some of my parents' friends. Inge and I were thrilled when the sky was suddenly filled with airplanes; however, I recall the glum look on my father's face and his friend's gloomy remark, "This doesn't look good." In the weeks that followed Trier was decorated in red, white, and black swastika banners. Chancellor Hitler would soon be paying a visit to the city and when he did, one of Inge's classmates would proudly shake his hand. On September 1, 1939, German troops marched into Poland and World War II began. I was just over 5 years old.

Perhaps the move to Trier had not been a good idea after all. My father became increasingly concerned for our safety. The city was very close to the Luxembourg and French borders from where, he knew, war was likely to come. I was too young to know about war, gathering only that once again we would have to leave our

Getting around in Trier

home, this time to Braunschweig on the train route between Hanover and Berlin.

My mother, with whatever help a 5 and an 8 year old could provide, packed all of our household belongings and we boarded the train east. Once again my father had gone ahead, having arranged to meet with a friend in the dairy business where he hoped to get a job. But his friend instead suggested a new opportunity. In the Nussberg woods outside Braunschweig was a popular restaurant owned by a brewery. The owners were looking for a new man to lease and manage the restaurant, and my father would apply for the position.

The large restaurant featured a beer garden that seated more than 1,000 guests, and it was packed with people on the Sunday of his visit. He was impressed by this "going concern." How could he lose? The next day he went to the brewery and after an interview was hired as the new lessor and manager of Restaurant

With one of Inge's girlfriends in Trier

The restaurant in the Nussberg was a busy place.

Nussberg, which would be our family business and home until 1961. Unfortunately, and to his lasting regret, to secure his job he would eventually be forced to join the party (the National Socialist Party) and wear the little swastika lapel pin. To my knowledge he never attended a party meeting or talked politics, but he did wear the little lapel pin. Had he not, there is no telling how our future would have unfolded. For now, he had made us secure and the little lapel pin seemed to be a small price to pay.

On the way to Braunschweig my mother, Inge, and I had stopped over in Hanover to see my aunt Hermine, whom we affectionately called "Tante Hermie." When my father called to tell us about the restaurant and his new job, my mother began to cry. It was not a life she looked forward to; her parents had owned a restaurant and she remembered the endless hours of hard work and drudgery. But my father had made the decision for all of us and so, once again, we boarded the train. Our next stop was Braunschweig, which was covered with snow when we arrived. My father met us at the train station and surprised Inge and me with our first sled.

Our new home would be located in the Restaurant Nussberg in a wooded valley some miles away from the city center of Braunschweig. There were three bedrooms on the second floor of the restaurant, one for my father and mother, one for Inge and me, and a third small room for one of our three housemaids. The other two housemaids shared a room on the third floor. On the ground floor were two kachelofen, the tile ovens that burned wood and coal to heat the house. One was in the restaurant, the other in our dining/living room. On another large wood-burning stove in our kitchen my mother cooked meals for our family and occasional hotel guests. The house had no running water and required pumping and carrying water from a well. For us it was a big house and so much better than the apartment in Trier. Still, Inge and I realized that, unlike Trier, we were out in the country and totally isolated. It would be difficult to make friends although both of us were immediately enrolled in the Heinrich Schule, my first grammar school, and would begin studies in a few days.

The building occupied by Restaurant Nussberg was originally built as an army guard station in 1865. Two years later it was enlarged to provide living space for officers. Although the exact date when the guard station was converted into a restaurant is unknown, we do know that in 1896 a man named Hermann Felten enlarged and improved the building for that purpose. The renovation included indoor and outdoor seating that would accommodate more than 1,000 guests. Musical concerts held every week during the summer attracted people from the city and surrounding areas.

In his history of Braunschweig, Burchardt Warnecke writes about the restaurant and its surroundings: "…the people in this beautiful area could enjoy nature and have a beautiful view of the heights of the mountains…. The children had no idea that from these mountains came the unique stone (Roggenstein) from which many of the important buildings like the cathedral in Braunschweig had been built."

Restaurant Nussberg served good food and beer at reasonable prices and would quickly gain a reputation as a meeting place for friends and families. Warnecke writes that the restaurant was a place where one could bring his own coffee and for 15 cents purchase hot water in a mug or a coffee can. A sign proclaimed, "Mit altem Brauch

Our new home in the Nussberg

Inside our restaurant-home

15 cents purchase hot water in a mug or a coffee can. A sign proclaimed, "Mit altem Brauch wird nicht gebrochen hier können Familien Kaffee kochen" (the old custom we will not break, family can brew coffee here). He goes on to say, "In 1940, the couple Albert and Alwine Fasterding [my parents] managed the restaurant. Guests affectionately called Mr. Fasterding 'the king of the Nussberg'." Indeed, Warnecke has done his research well!

Our family had moved twice in my father's attempt to keep us out of harm's way and to earn a living in the months leading up to Germany's declaration of war in 1939. Now we seemed to be settled in the restaurant business. Time and again my fathers' friends had tried to persuade him to join the National Socialist Party of Adolf Hitler, and time and again he had refused. He had lost his business in Berka because he was not a party member. In those days people were forced to choose – you were either a Bolshevik or a Nazi. Now, in 1940, in order to have the job at the restaurant, he had no choice. He wore the little National Socialist pin in his lapel but never believed. He had deep-seated reasons for his beliefs and was not willing to compromise his principles.

A summer evening at Restaurant Nussberg

CHAPTER TWO

MY FATHER

"'Do you have anything from him, any papers?' 'I have only a single postcard,' replied Hermine. 'Bring it to me at the embassy,' said the Ambassador."

ALBERT HEINRICH WILHELM FASTERDING WAS BORN IN
GROSSHIMSTEDT, LOWER SAXONY, ON AUGUST 7, 1893. He was the
second youngest of 10 children, only 1 year older than his youngest sister. His mother,
Sofie, died when he was just 2 ½ years old, and their father would die when Albert was
11. His oldest sister, Hermine, just a teenager, became mother to the nine Fasterding
children. Her bond with Albert would, in later years, change his life.

My father told us how he worked, first on his family farm and then in his family inn
and restaurant, precursors to a career in later life that he could not imagine at the time.
He was a good student and was singled out to help teach the younger children in his
school. He left school at age 16 and although one of his teachers encouraged him to go
to Braunschweig and enroll in a school to study the dairy business, he was unable to
do so for at least 2 years because his help was needed on the family farm. At age 18 he
did go to Braunschweig to enroll in the dairy school.

Then in 1914, on a beautiful spring day in the far-away Serbian city of Sarajevo, a
single pistol shot fired by a young revolutionary killed the Archduke Franz Ferdinand.

The alliances in force among European countries plunged the world into war. Very soon 20-year-old Albert Fasterding and thousands of young German boys were off to the French front where he was wounded and evacuated to a hospital in Insterburg, East Prussia.

As the tide of war changed and Albert recovered from the bullet wound in his leg, he was sent back into battle, this time to the Eastern Front where things were not going well for the Germans. With many others he was taken prisoner by the Russians and shipped off to Stavropol in the Caucuses. Along the way the train stopped to allow the prisoners to relieve themselves, and young Albert was persuaded by a friend to make a run to escape. A guard was watching and did not hesitate; he raised his rifle and shot my father, again in the leg. He and his fellow prisoners were loaded back aboard the cattle car and the train continued to the prison camp in Stavropol.

For the next 10 years Stavropol would be Albert's home. He would work in a coal mine, do road construction, and perform other hard labor. He was resourceful, could fix electrical systems and repair broken pipes, and soon became known as a "jack of all trades." He was a model prisoner.

In 1918 when the Russians installed a flour mill and had no one to operate it, my father was their man. During this time of the Bolshevik Revolution, he recalled watching a Red (Bolshevik) Russian enter the mill and kill his own brother, a White

My father (far left) in the hospital at Insterburg, East Prussia

Russian who believed in the monarchy, in capitalism, and in an alternative form of socialism. When the war was over and the prisoners were sent home, Albert stayed on even though he was a free man. For the remainder of his time in Russia he managed the mill while his brothers and sisters knew nothing of his whereabouts or his condition. It had been more than 2 years since his family had heard from him. Back in 1916, before his capture, they had received one postcard that he had written from the Eastern front.

In Germany, Albert's sister Hermine continued her role as matriarch of the family, never knowing what had become of her little brother. She was young and beautiful and in time married Reinhold Polzin (our "Uncle Holdi"), a successful lawyer who became a judge. The couple moved to Berlin where they became well known in the social circles of post-war society.

In 1924 it was not at all unusual that this stylish couple would be invited one evening to a glamorous dinner party in honor of the Russian Ambassador to Germany. It was unusual and a complete matter of chance, however, that Hermine was seated next to the Ambassador. In a conversation about families she mentioned that her youngest brother had been captured years ago by the Russians and had vanished during his captivity. The family knew only that he had been detained at a camp in the Caucasus

My father with fellow prisoners in Stavropol

My father as foreman of the mill

Tante Hermi, my father's oldest sister, with her husband, Reinhold (Onkel Holdi)

Tante Hermi and Onkel Holdi

Mountains. The Ambassador was curious: "Do you have anything from him, any papers?" "I have only a single postcard," replied Hermine. "Bring it to me at the embassy."

As it turned out, the postcard showed Albert together with a group of other soldiers, and he had written his army identification number on the card. Tante Hermi took the postcard to the Russian embassy and with the Ambassador's help, the search began. Amazingly, when she heard back from the Ambassador, she learned not only that her brother was alive but also that he would soon be released as a result of the Ambassador's personal intervention.

The Ambassador learned that when other prisoners had been released from the camp, my father had agreed to stay on to manage the mill. He learned too that

Tante Hermi, a stylish
lady

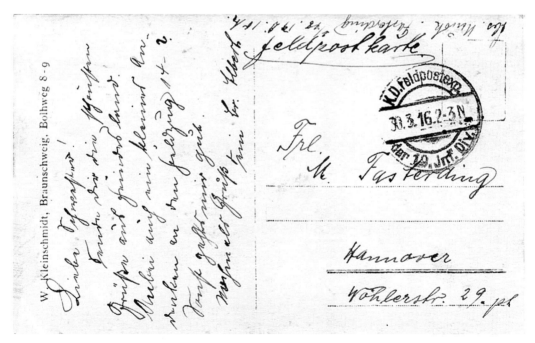

The clue that led to my father's release

my father spoke Russian, that he had a girlfriend who was a teacher, and that they were engaged to be married. Perhaps Albert had thought he would stay on in Russia because he had heard things were hopeless in Germany. But when word arrived that his sister was responsible for his release, he knew he had to go home.

"…he had a girlfriend who was a teacher, and … they were engaged to be married."

My father and his Russian girlfriend

Those who managed the mill had grown fond of my father and had presented him with a silver embossed wallet and some money as a good-bye present. In addition, the Ambassador had arranged for him to be paid for his services as mill foreman. So Albert left Stavropol for home with enough money to visit a variety of Russian cities along the way, including Moscow. There was no further mention of his Russian girlfriend when he arrived in Berlin for a happy reunion with Hermine and later with his other sisters and brothers.

Albert arrives home

"Workers of the World Unite – A. Fasterdyng from the staff of district Golniza, SSSR, 14th of April, 1926"
[They had misspelled his name!]

"This currently dated certificate is issued to Fasterding, Albert in as much
as he served in state farm Number 8 from the 5th of October 22 year,
to the 15th of March 23 year in the position of a mechanic at a mill and
dairy which the below signature and application of seal verifies."

CHAPTER THREE
MY MOTHER

"Alwine Schlieker [Fasterding], one of eight
children, was born December 28, 1906."

The traditional German village of 300 inhabitants where my mother was born and grew up

ALWINE SCHLIEKER, ONE OF EIGHT CHILDREN, WAS BORN DECEMBER 28, 1906, IN THE SMALL AND CHARMING LOWER SAXONY VILLAGE OF WARBSEN. Her parents, Johanne and Wilhelm, owned and operated "Gasthof Schlieker," the special inn that was also their family home. From my childhood visits I remember the cozy beer room and the walls covered with deer antlers and the prominently displayed painting of the house. A large wood-burning kachelofen provided heat, and an open cabinet filled with schnaps sat above a beer barrel. In the evening the room was filled with men from the village who came to smoke their pipes and drink beer. After working in the fields and on the farm during

My grandparents' home, restaurant, inn, and bank

My grandfather, Wilhelm Schlieker, from his time in WW I to when I knew him

the day, the Schlieker children worked for their parents in this village gathering place in the evening.

In the fall, when many came to Warbsen to hunt wild boar and deer in the nearby fields and forests, the Gasthof Schlieker was a favored place to stay. To make room for the guests, the Schlieker children often shared rooms. All manner of village celebrations were held in the upstairs ballroom; the inn also contained a bank branch office of which my grandfather was the manager. At one time, he was also the mayor of Warbsen. For years the Gasthof Schlieker was the center of village activity, and Wilhelm Schlieker was the man in charge.

My grandfather also owned and farmed many hectares of land that included pastures, cornfields, potato fields, and woods. He raised cows, goats, pigs, and chickens; cultivated a large vegetable garden; and fished in the river that flowed behind the garden. I remember all of these details from 1941 and 1942, when our mother took Inge and me for 2- to 3-week visits to the farm in Warbsen during our summer vacations from school. We collected eggs, picked vegetables with my grandmother, and brought in the cut wood for the fire. My grandmother taught me to knit and kneed bread. I remember that we once tried to turn the huge wooden bread trough into a boat, which sank when we got into it. Connected to the inn was a barn with a very

Flash forward to 1942 with our cousins in Warbsen for vacation

large round door through which my grandfather would guide the cows or a big wagon full of clover or hay as Inge and I perched on top.

If you were to go to Warbsen today, you would see the village much as it was when my grandfather and grandmother lived there. A building that looks very much like a church still stands in the center of the village; in those days it also contained the one-room grammar school. Gasthof Schlieker is now a family home. Many of the houses still standing in Warbsen are of the traditional design dating back hundreds of years. They are so classic that in later years wealthy people had them taken apart and moved to new locations in Braunschweig and other cities. They can still be visited in those locations today.

My mother left Warbsen for the first time when she was 16 or 17. Like the other Schlieker girls, she was sent to an estate owned by Baron von Schulenburg near Hamelin. Yes, this was the same Hamelin

My mother (center) at the von Schulenburg estate

Family harvest time at the Schlieker farm

My father's graduating class at the dairy college

The engagement of Albert and Alwine

of legendary "Pied Piper" fame. Here, in this incredible chateau, surrounded by beautiful gardens and a moat, young Alwine Schlieker was apprenticed to the manager of the household. She learned all manner of housekeeping skills including cooking, washing, ironing, and embroidery (for her future dowry). On her return, my mother worked in the inn and the fields and, as the second oldest daughter, took care of her younger brother and three younger sisters.

My parents' wedding, November 30, 1930

My parents' wedding, November 30, 1930

Then one day in 1928 a young handsome man named Albert Fasterding came to stay at Gasthof Schlieker. After 10 years in a Russian prison camp he had been released in 1926, to rejoin his sister in Berlin. With her help he had travelled to Braunschweig to continue his studies of the dairy business in the school there. On graduation from the school in Braunschweig he had been sent to Warbsen to apprentice in the local dairy company.

I know nothing about their first encounter, only that the courtship went on for 2 years without the approval of my grandparents. After all, their daughter was only 24 and this Fasterding fellow was an "old" man of 37. Yes he had a job at the dairy, but he was without any real money. Yet somehow he overcame their objections and on November 30, 1930, Albert Fasterding and Alwine Schlieker were married in a ceremony at Gasthof Schlieker. Their wedding picture shows a large gathering of the family, and of course the most important people of the village were also

Inge's first picture

in attendance.

Soon after the wedding Albert secured a position as manager of a small dairy in the nearby village of Berka. As part of the new position, they were provided rooms upstairs at the dairy. Here in their first home on November 3, 1931, my sister, Inge Marlis Gerda, was born.

Even with a young baby who needed constant care, my mother continued to tend to the household chores, while my father was in the dairy making butter and managing the enterprise. So when it was time for me to be born, my father took his wife to a hospital in Northeim for some well-deserved rest. There I was born at noon on Sunday April 8, 1934. I had come into a world on the brink of turmoil; my life was to be shaped by the tumultuous events of the next decade.

Two years before I was born, in 1932, Adolf Hitler had become a German citizen in what was to become my home town of Braunschweig because Hitler

First picture of me

had not been able to participate in German politics as an Austrian. In January of 1933, he became Chancellor of Germany. Although he had come to power legally, he quickly and brutally transformed the German state into his personal dictatorship with a vendetta against all Jews. A frightened world waited to see what would come next as leaders on both sides of the Atlantic opted to stay out of the affairs of Germany.

Then, in 1934, with the death of Chancellor Hindenburg, the Chancellorship and Presidency of the country were united in the person of Adolf Hitler. He became "the Führer" and all aspects of government, law, and education became appendages of his National Socialist Party. Soon the entire country was caught up in Hitler worship. Millions of Germans welcomed the new nationalism despite struggling under reparation payments to the victors of World War I and being threatened by hyperinflation, political turmoil, and a potential Communist takeover. The obligatory form of greeting was "Heil Hitler!," and before long little boys and girls would salute their "Führer" along with their parents and grandparents.

cutline

CHAPTER FOUR

WHEN THE BOMBS BEGAN TO FALL

"Every day our teachers would tell us that Germany was the most powerful country in the world and that surely the war would be over by Christmas."

My first day at school

I WAS 6 YEARS OLD IN THE SPRING OF 1940 — A HEADY TIME FOR THE NEW GERMAN NATIONALISM. By early May France, Holland, Belgium, and Luxembourg had fallen to Hitler's advancing legions. By the end of the month Germans cheered another victory as 338,000 desperate British and French forces were miraculously evacuated from the beaches at Dunkirk. In June more German victories were reported in Lithuania, Latvia, and Estonia, and on June 27, with Nazi troops occupying Paris, France capitulated. As Germany conquered country after country, Inge and I were happy little girls. Every day our teacher would tell us that Germany was the most powerful country in the world and that surely "the war would be over by Christmas!" We believed her.

Braunschweig had become home to numerous units of the German military machine. Paratroopers were stationed not far from our restaurant in the Nussberg; the Luftwaffe had an installation there as did the Wehrmacht. There was even a special high school in the town castle, the "Junker Schule." It was operated exclusively for brilliant students ages 14-18 who on graduation would become members of the "SS." These groups never mingled with each other but individually held parties and balls at Restaurant Nussberg. Despite his disagreement with the national policy and the war, my father operated the restaurant on a professional basis.

Our living quarters in the restaurant were still very "basic." My mother was often in tears because we had no water, except what came from the outside well. There was no heat except for the two huge kachelofen in which we burned wood or coal during the day. Upstairs, where everyone dressed, there was just one little stove. In the winter my mother prepared the fire in the evening and lit it in the morning so we could have a little heat to get dressed for school. Often she filled a stone bottle (schnapsflasche) with hot water and put it in our bed at night. The worst thing was that we had to go outdoors to the bathroom even when it was very cold.

That April of 1940 I had started school. The first couple of times my mother took me to the "Heinrich Schule," about a 15- or 20-minute walk from home, and then Inge and I walked together. I always carried a little backpack called a "Tournister," which contained a slate and a sponge to clean it. My books were simple ABC books. I remember we had to write each of the letters over and over again to cover the slate: first the big A and the small one, then the alphabet, and then words. When Inge was 10 she went on to the "Lyzeum Kleine Burg" (the all-girls' high school) and I walked to school alone. As I said, we were isolated out there in the Nussberg, with no neighbors and no other students with whom to walk to school.

I enjoyed school. Many of my girlfriends came to the Nussberg after school to play games like "Robbers and Police." When we "police" caught a "robber," we tied him to a tree, gave him a sugar cube to keep him quiet, and put a big handkerchief over his mouth for good measure before going after more robbers.

It was around this time that my Mother sent Inge and me to a music school to learn to play the piano. I loved the piano but not the teacher. I often came home from my lesson in tears and when my mother asked why, I did not want to tell her. She persisted and so I finally explained that when I made a mistake the teacher hit my fingers with a stick. My mother immediately took us out of the music school and found a private teacher — Edith Löhnefinke — with whom we could continue our studies. In my lessons I had an especially difficult time with the rhythm of the waltz, and she would crank up the record player and dance with me. Miss Löhnefinke left an indelible impression on me because together we would go round and round until I would finally get it right. I adored her and thought of her then as being very old — maybe even 50!

In the spring of 1941, when I was 7, French prisoners of war who were held in a nearby camp built a bunker exclusively for a select group of people — the" Brown Shirts," the Mayor of Braunschweig and his staff, high-ranking military officers, and selected

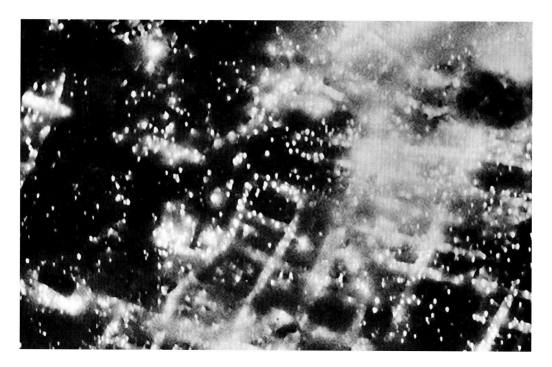

Bombs lit up the night and Braunschweig was on fire.

others. A second bunker, right next to the first, was for police headquarters. Even when the bombs began to fall, these bunkers were "off limits" for the general population. Once these "special" bunkers were finished, the prisoners built one large bunker with multiple entrances to protect the citizens of Braunschweig from the expected Allied bombing. For our family, however, those bunkers brought an unexpected bonus: one of them required a waterline that also served our restaurant and house. For the first time, we had running water and did not have to use our pump. What a blessing!

That summer on the 17th of August, when excavation for the bunker near us had just begun, we had an unexpected opportunity to explore it. Inge and I were in bed when we began to hear the anti-aircraft guns that had been placed around the city. As the sounds grew louder and louder we got out of bed, put on the black warm-up suits we always kept close by, and came downstairs. My father was sitting with a couple in the Gaststube and my mother was sewing in the living/dining room. They were surprised to see us and said, "Go back to bed, we live in the woods; no plane will find us here." But we stayed downstairs on the couch with our mother and a short time later heard the first bomb coming down. It hit right out in front between the restaurant and the new bunker, and the sound was terrible.

With the explosion my father said, "Let's go to the bunker!" and he left with the

There would be two bunkers like this one built not for the citizens of Braunschweig but for "special" people. Most of the many rooms in the bunker were located deep underground.

couple. We waited for our housemaids to come downstairs, and they were in their nightgowns and bare feet. The bomb had shaken the house and the restaurant and there were broken beer glasses everywhere. Before we could leave we had to get shoes for the housemaids so they would not cut their feet. Finally, when it was quiet, we left the house and headed for the bunker. We had to skirt the bomb crater out front; it was wide and deep. One piece of the bomb had gone right through the door of our storage room. We kept that piece of shrapnel as a reminder.

The bunker was deep underground. The 20- to 30-foot-long passageways were lined with stone and were very wet. Eight of us just stood there thinking we were safe underground when more planes came with more bombs. The man with my father was a soldier in uniform, and I remember him pointing to a fire in the ballroom of the restaurant. My father wanted to rush out to save the building but it was not safe. When the soldier looked again he said, "The fire has gone out." Later we would find that a small incendiary bomb had come through the roof and rested against a broken glass window before burning itself out without doing any real damage. Finally we heard a very long siren, the "all clear," and we went back to the restaurant.

From that night on we lived in fear. American bombers came during the day and British bombers at night. Braunschweig was clearly a major target on the bomber run from Hanover to Berlin. My father had always told us that we were safe in the Nussberg and that they could not find us in the forest; but he was wrong. We did not know it at the time, but seven people were killed the night of that first raid. In the months and years ahead many more would die. Like other German cities, Braunschweig was an allied target. Between this first attack and the end of the war, there would be 42 bombing raids. I later learned that a number of factories in and around Braunschweig were making war materials including bomb sights, and that Braunschweig was the garrison city for the 31st Infantry Division of the German army. These were the troops who took part in the invasions of Poland, Belgium, France, and Russia.

Soon our family had our own personal bunker, built by hand by my father and our housemaid who, like many other Russian girls, had been taken from her home by the German government to work in Germany. We called her "Schura" but her real name was "Alexandra," and she was very strong and a good worker. In Russia she had carried railroad ties on a construction site. We all loved Schura and were happy to have her as a member of the family.

Our Schura

I listened to our radio as often as I could and finally figured out the bombing patterns. When the Americans and the British were bombing Hanover or another city west of Braunschweig, a distinct preliminary alarm whined very slowly. On hearing it mothers and children prepared to go to the bunker. Then as the sound became faster and faster, people at work would leave their jobs and head for the bunker. If I had been listening to the radio when the siren stopped, I would run to the public bunker and tell everyone that they could all go home because the airplanes had dropped their bombs on Hanover or another city to the west of us.

One day as I was on my way to the bunker with the "news," I was stopped by one of the brown shirts. "What are you doing?" he demanded. When I explained that I was bringing news about the bombing to the west of us so the people could go

My family: Spring 1943

home, he said, "You are a very good German girl; are you in the Hitler Youth?" I said I was not but that I could hardly wait to join because I had heard stories from my friends at school that it was a lot of fun. He said I should follow him to the SA bunker and so I did, not thinking that this might not be a very good idea. The entrance was built like a maze, twisting and turning before it emptied into a very long red-carpeted hallway.

The walls of the first two rooms were covered with huge maps and little swastika flags indicating the presence of German troops. There were big desks, and in a couple of the rooms people wore earphones. I guess they were radio operators. At the end of the long corridor was a snack bar where the guard lifted me up on a high chair and a very pretty lady behind

The foreman grabbed me by my pigtails!

the bar opened a big flat box filled with chocolates. The guard said that I could help myself, so I did and I think I ate half the box. I could not believe my eyes — I had never seen chocolates like that! Before I left he led me into one of the card rooms

My uncle Helmut. All little 10 year olds were required to join Hitler Youth.

like that! Before I left he led me into one of the card rooms where there was a library. He took two books off the shelf and gave them to me.

My parents thought it was good that the guard had rewarded me for doing good work. I still remember the little round table with a shelf on which we kept those books throughout the war. I could not read them at the time of course, but I still have them — illustrated books on German history and archeology.

One day I was on my way home from school when I saw a large group of people doing road work and wearing what I thought were pajamas. Each of them wore a cap with a number on it, and when I listened to them talking, I was amazed to hear them speaking German! At home I asked my parents, "What are all those people doing here, and if they are prisoners, why are they speaking German?" My father said they were Jews and Christians who were against the regime and so had to work. He never explained where they came from or why they "had to work." I guess he thought I was too young to understand.

French and Italian prisoners were also working on the bunkers near our house. On Saturday and Sunday evenings they wandered by the restaurant, not to eat or drink but just to take a look. Just 2 minutes away was the bunker for the "Brown shirts," the SA people, and I remember taking some bread from the restaurant to trade for chocolate. I knew that the French prisoners working on the bunker received boxes of food and chocolate from France. They seemed to be treated fairly, and my sister and I really liked

We did not believe my father; we believed our teachers.

them. Unhappily, while I got my chocolate I also got caught by one of the guards! He grabbed me by my pigtails and slapped me in the face. He said I was a terrible little girl and should never talk to prisoners.

In November of 1941 Inge turned ten and was invited, or I should say required, to join the "Bund Deutscher Mädchen" (BDM) or "Hitler Youth." They met once a week on Wednesdays after school. When she came home she told me how they visited orphanages and old people's homes where they sang folk songs. They made little toys for the orphan children and learned to knit "Pulswärmer" to keep the soldiers' wrists warm. It sounded like a lot of fun. I admired her uniform and could not wait to become a member.

Germany was fighting on two fronts in 1943. Radio broadcasts were filled with propaganda about how well everything was going. In school our teacher told us how Germany had marched into Norway, Denmark, Holland, and Belgium; and we all sang "Deutschland, Deutschland über Alles." We were very proud of our country.

Each day our teacher reported on how well the war was going and how important it was that we all become part of the war effort, so as patriotic little Germans we collected lots of things for the Führer. We searched the sides of the road for herbs to make tea and animal bones to make soap. We looked for tin, paper, and discarded clothing. We took all of these things to school where they were collected. Because there was no

A Nazi rally in the Thingplatz

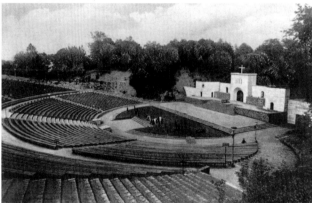

The Thingplatz in more peaceful times

pesticide we were asked to go into the potato fields to pick the bugs off the potato plants. What an awful job that was!

One day Inge and I had just come home from school and were celebrating the news of the most recent victory of Germany as reported by our teachers. When my father overheard us he said, "Girls, come here," and he gathered us around the dining room table. He then spread out a map of the world in front of us, pointed with his finger, and said, "Girls, this is the United States, this is Russia, and this tiny little country here is Germany! How can we possibly win this war?" We both were very angry with him because we were being taught very differently, and we believed our teachers.

The Americans and the British had identified numerous targets in and around the Braunschweig city center including machine and munitions works, the nearby harbor, research institutions, railway stations, and maintenance works, along with the German Research Center for Aviation. As the bombings intensified, parents sent their children away to relatives or friends in villages far from the city. The administration gathered all of the high school kids together and, for their safety, shipped them by train to the Hartz Mountains. Inge was among them. She was eleven and a half and I was nine. I would miss her very much.

As it turns out, I was allowed to stay home because of my age and because my father had spoken to a friend who was a medical doctor. He had explained that Inge had already left and I was too young and fragile to endure such a journey. The doctor had composed a memorandum to the authorities advising that despite the bombings, I should stay home with my parents.

Even with the constant fear of bombs, our restaurant was filled with guests almost every evening. Many came to be close to the bunker, just in case. A friend and I provided the entertainment, presenting plays and skits. I played a fancy lady, a minister, and a clown. As I mentioned, most restaurant guests came from the city and stayed until the alarm sounded, when they headed to the bunker.

On a hillside very near our restaurant was the "Thingplatz," a huge outdoor amphitheater that held close to 2,000 people. It had been used for theatrical performances and even church services, but when the Nazis came to Braunschweig, they renovated it for the patriotic rallies that were held mostly at night with torches, a band, and huge banners.

My father and I, age 9, in my jump suit, just in case

Many such letters were written during Inge's evacuation.

Friday, 29.9. 1944

My dear, good parents, sweet little Matzele,

I received your dear letter of 25.9 yesterday. Many hearty thanks. Today I have for the third time tried to get a telephone call through to you. The day before yesterday I waited five hours but nothing came through. Yesterday morning before breakfast I tried to make another telephone attempt and at nine in the evening the operator said the receiving person doesn't answer. Today I tried again. Is your telephone broken down? I'm so frightened not to hear anything from you and I could really cry.

Here, one said, that the bomb attack was in Braunschweig. Is that true? Yesterday noon we had a two and a half hour alarm. A huge group of airplanes flew over us and we all had terrible fear. Many flew in the direction of Braunschweig.

The day before yesterday we were given vacation until the 11.October. We were all delighted about that. Unfortunately we are not allowed to travel. Now I wanted to ask you on my telephone call when you, my dearest little sister, will come; and who will bring you? Please come soon so that you will be here when they have visiting day. It would be a pity if you could not see our fairy tale and short play. You can sleep at Hagemeisters. Oh, you have no idea how much I am longing for you and look forward to your visit.

Now, during the vacation, they wake us up at 8 o'clock. Undoubtedly there will soon be an alarm as there are eight barrage balloons in the sky. It would be a pity if we have to stay the whole day in the cellar. We often have alarms now.

I hope our house is now repaired, or is the roof not yet covered? I wish that the terror bombing would not destroy everything. But we have never been lucky.

What pity that your telephone is not working. I am so pleased that the bombed out festival hall at our restaurant will be built again. Hopefully we can see one another very very soon. Please let me hear something from you soon.

In great longing, many thousands of hearty greetings and millions of kisses,

Your loving Inge

Once I noticed them preparing for a rally, putting up banners, and arranging the stage. I went closer to watch and saw that they were hanging Japanese banners next to the swastikas because the Japanese foreign minister was visiting Braunschweig. I had learned at school that the Japanese were our allies and that they were going to help us win the war, so I wanted to see the stadium. I was 10 but had not yet become a member of the Hitler Youth.

80,000 people were bombed out of their homes.

I continued to walk to school in the city. By now all schools had been bombed out or closed, leaving only a collective school for boys and girls of all ages, which was twice the walk as my grammar school. These students, like me, were permitted to stay home with their parents for a variety of medical reasons. Although the school had not yet been bombed, we all sensed it would only be a matter of time.

Around noon on a beautiful day in May, when the chestnut trees were in bloom and we all were in school, the alarm began to whine and the teacher quickly directed us all down into the basement. We left our books behind and clamored down the stairs. The basement was very dark and the air was stifling because the half windows onto the street had been blockaded with sandbags. Suddenly we were hit by a phosphorous bomb that created billows of smoke. We all screamed as we heard the beams above us crack and break. We thought we would be burned alive as we knew many people in Braunschweig had been. Outside several old men began to move the sandbags away

from the windows and one by one they pulled us out. I remember being pulled out by one of the old men, and as soon as I was on the street I ran for home. Home was 20 minutes away, and I never stopped, never looked back. I did look left and right to make sure nothing would fall on me from the burning houses as I passed, but I had only one thought – to get home and see my parents! I burst through the door and they took me in their arms. I was so happy to be safe and to know they were safe too. That was the last day that I would attend school in the city.

My father had received permission for me to stay at home, but only if I would go on my bicycle to a village school about 4 miles away, in Rautheim. Only the children of farmers went to this school, and they did not like me because I was a city girl and knew so much more than they. The boys were impressed, however, because when we played high jump, I could jump higher than anyone in the class. We took turns listening to the radio and when we heard that the bombers were headed for Hanover, the teacher would say, "Marlis, you can go home now." So I would hop on my bicycle for the 20-minute ride home. One of those days, I was almost home when bombs began to fall just a few yards from me. Frightened and shaking, I steered my bike into a ditch, ducked down, and waited until the planes were gone. When things had quieted down, I pulled myself together and pedalled home.

Our restaurant continued to be the center of activity in the Nussberg; my father managed to keep it running night after night throughout the war. On Sundays, when some of the Russian prisoners were given time off, they would come to the restaurant. They knew my father spoke Russian and that they were very likely to get something to eat. My mother hid cooked potatoes with the skins on for the prisoners to find near the water pump outside the restaurant and instead of eating them, they put them in their pockets to take back to the camp. They liked my father and did not want him to get in trouble because they had been caught eating near the restaurant. He told them he knew how it felt to be a prisoner of war, he talked with them about their lives in Germany, and he told them about his experience in Russia those many years ago. Nevertheless, such fraternization with prisoners was dangerous, and one night two Nazi SA officers came to the restaurant and took my father to the bunker for questioning. As I remember, he was kept overnight while my mother and I were told nothing and were scared. As it turns out, a local person in the bunker spoke out to support my father and, with a warning not to do it again, he was released. My father was very well liked by the people of the Nussberg.

"Inge and her classmates wrote postcards and letters home describing how they kept track of the American and British bombers by watching their routes overhead. They were constantly worried for their families."

Inge would be away for 1 ½ years. She went off on a train full of students with their luggage. She later told us that when they arrived at what would be their home and school in the Hartz Mountains, there was no train station. The train just stopped near the town of Beneckenstein where they climbed out and up a long, very steep bank to a former pension or bed and breakfast in Hohegeis. Their teacher, Frau Oppermann, stayed with them, and they went to school from eight in the morning until one in the afternoon. While the owners of the house stayed downstairs and cooked for the girls, two young BDM girls helped Frau Opperman. During that year and a half it was nearly impossible for the children to make a telephone call home because the telephones that did work were almost always busy. Inge and her classmates wrote postcards and letters home describing how they kept track of the American and British bombers by watching their routes overhead. They were constantly worried for their families.

For Inge away in the mountains and for me in Braunschweig, June 6, 1944 — "D-Day"— was just another day. How could we have known that on that day, thousands of allied troops and machinery were storming ashore along the French coast at Normandy? Although it was the greatest invasion force the world had ever seen, how

Freitag, 14. Oktober 1994 **FEUERSTURM ÜBER BRAUNSCHWEIG**

Blick von der Andreaskirche hinab auf das Trümmerfeld der Innenstadt. Rechts die Weberstraße. Das Weichbild Neustadt gehörte zu den am meisten betroffenen Gebieten beim Angriff britischer Bomber am 15. Oktober 1944.

Die Poststraße. Auch das Gewandhaus ist ausgebrannt. Anfangs stand der Giebel noch, aber bei Sturm stürzte später das ausgeglühte Mauerwerk herab.

Die Sonnenstraße mit der Martinikirche: Soldaten räumen den Weg frei.

Bombenhagel und Feuersturm: 633 Tote

80 000 ohne Obdach

4500 Männer der Feuerwehr, etwa 1000 Männer und Frauen der Luftschutzdienste und dazu Einheiten der Wehrmacht waren in der Nacht des 15. Oktober und in den Tagen danach im Einsatz. Den Braunschweiger Feuerwehren waren Kräfte aus der näheren und weiteren Umgebung zu Hilfe gekommen — aus Salzgitter, Peine, Hannover, Gifhorn und Goslar, aber auch aus Hildesheim, Blankenburg, Wernigerode und Quedlinburg. Erst am 20. Oktober fuhren die letzten dieser Einheiten in ihre Heimatorte zurück.

Sie verließen eine Stadt, deren Zentrum zu 90 Prozent zerstört und schwer beschädigt war. 80 000 Menschen waren obdachlos geworden. Die Zahl der Todesopfer in diesem Feuersturm konnte nie mit letzter Sicherheit ermittelt werden. In den Zeitungen erschienen täglich neue Zahlen. Am 4. Dezember meldete die „Braunschweiger Tageszeitung" (BTZ) 633 Tote, wobei sie sorgfältig unterschied zwischen „596 Gefallenen" und „weiterhin" 37 Ausländern, die „den Tod fanden". Diese Zahl — rund sieben Wochen nach dem Angriff veröffentlicht — dürfte gültig sein. Insgesamt verloren bei Luftangriffen auf Braunschweig 2905 Menschen das Leben.

Notmaßnahmen waren seit langem vorbereitet. In den über die ganze Stadt verteilten Auffangstellen wurden die „Ausgebombten" zunächst untergebracht und verpflegt. Nächste Station waren die Betreuungsstellen des „Sozialamtes für Fliegergeschädigte". Elf sicherer Stellen waren am Stadtrand eingerichtet. Hier gab es neue Ausweise, Geld, Lebensmittelkarten und „Bombenpässe", die zum Bezug bestimmter Waren oder auch zum Erhalt von Dienstleistungen berechtigten. In Großsammelstellen wurden die Obdachlosen aufgenommen, bis ihnen neuer Wohnraum zugewiesen werden konnte.

Die Abteilung „Hausratsicherung" innerhalb des „Sozialamtes für Fliegergeschädigte" stellte später Bergungs- und Transportpersonal sowie Lagerräume für Möbel aus schwer beschädigten Häusern zur Verfügung.

Die Verpflegung kam aus Feld- und Großküchen. Zur Unterstützung reisten sogenannte „Hilfszüge" an. Autokolonnen mit Küche, Fachpersonal und ausreichend Geschirr, die schnell große Menschenmassen abfertigen konnten. Sonst aber war die Versorgung der Bevölkerung äußerst schwierig. Von 215 Schlachtereien waren nur 58 und von 210 Bäckereien nur etwa 90 übriggeblieben. Die BTZ vom 17. Oktober veröffentlichte die Firmennamen von nur elf geöffneten Lebensmittelgeschäften.

Es gab zunächst kein Wasser, kein Gas und keinen Strom. Tankwagen brachten Trinkwasser heran. Auf Dauer konnte die Stadt nicht mit 80 000 obdachlosen Menschen fertigwerden. So begann nur wenige Tage nach dem Angriff eine große Umsiedlungsaktion. Alle Ausgebombten, die nicht in Braunschweig ihren Arbeitsplatz hatten — also Mütter mit Kindern und alte Leute —, wurden mit Bussen und Sonderzügen in schon lange vorher festgelegte Evakuierungsgebiete gebracht. Es sollte bei manchen Jahre dauern, bis sie wieder zurückkehren konnten.

Radar unwirksam

Deutsche Abwehr ausgetrickst

Mehr als 1200 britische Bomber waren in der Nacht des 14./15. Oktober 1944 gegen Duisburg und Braunschweig als Hauptziele gestartet. Braunschweig war durch schwere Flak geschützt. Die Stellungen waren: Abtstraße, Lünischteich, Melverode, Ölper, Broitzem, Bürgerpark und Eintrachtstadion (später Lamme). In dieser Nacht schoß die Braunschweiger Flak jedoch nur einen Bomber ab. Insgesamt verlor das Bomberkommando nur neun Maschinen. Ein Fiasko für die deutsche Luftabwehr. Wie konnte es dazu kommen?

Die 100. Gruppe, die britische Sondereinheit, brachte in dieser Nacht alles in die Luft, was greifbar war: Stirling-Maschinen setzten mit „Mandrel"-Sendern das Küstenradar in Nordholland und Nordwestdeutschland außer Wirkung. Düppel (Stanniolstreifen) wurden bis hin zur Küste Schleswigs abgeworfen, um einen Angriff auf Hamburg vorzutäuschen. Scheinangriffe erfolgten gegen Helgoland, Mannheim und Düsseldorf. Auf diese Weise wurde die deutsche Luftabwehr total ausgetrickst.

Und so konnte dann im „The Bomber Command War Diaries" notiert werden: „Viermal wurde versucht, Braunschweig zu zerstören. Die 5. Gruppe erreichte dieses Ziel schließlich in dieser Nacht, indem sie ihre eigenen Markierungsmethoden benutzte. Verläßliche Statistiken über den Schaden sind spärlich. Anstatt die normale Zahl der zerstörten Gebäude anzugeben, wurde die Zerstörung in Hektar gemessen. Man erwähnt 150 Hektar der historischen Stadtfläche."

Ein Amerikaner schrieb

Bitte um Verzeihung

Vor längerer Zeit bereits traf ein Brief aus den USA im Rathaus ein. Frank M. Clark aus dem US-Staat Wisconsin, ehemaliger Bombenflieger, hat sich mit ihm bei den „Menschen, die in Braunschweig wohnen", Jahrzehnten „öffentlich entschuldigt, an einem Bombenangriff auf Ihre Stadt am 22. Oktober 1944 teilgenommen zu haben."

In dem Brief an die Stadtverwaltung heißt es weiter: „Als Soldaten wurde uns auf beiden Seiten befohlen, unsere Pflicht zu tun. Das bedeutet nicht, daß wir nicht teilhaben können an dem, was andere gefühlt haben. Wir müssen bedenken, daß Menschen, weil sie davon entfernt sind, perfekt zu sein, und im Umgang miteinander viele Fehler machen..."

Der jährlich auch in den USA begangene Volkstrauertag, schreibt Frank M. Clark, sollte Gelegenheit dafür bieten, begangenes Unrecht zu vergeben.

Fotos: Stadtarchiv Braunschweig, Städtisches Museum, Royal Air Force Museum (Hendon), Archiv Diestelmann, Archiv Grote, Könneke Sammlung Kalenberg. Farbfoto vom Gemälde „Brennendes Braunschweig" in der Nord/LB: Otto Hoppe.

Die Neue Straße, von der Gördelingerstraße aus gesehen. Links das Geschäftshaus von Pfeiffer & Schmidt. Heute ist dort die Dresdner Bank. Hinten rechts ist der Dom sichtbar. An der Ecke steht dort jetzt der Karstadt-Komplex.

Trotz Sandsäcken und Verschalung geschmolzen: der Altstadtmarkt-Brunnen.

An anniversary remembrance of the bombing of Braunschweig

could we know that June 6 marked the turning point in the war we had always been told we were winning? *And how could I know that one of those soldiers – Dick Grout – who came ashore at Normandy would, one day, become a dear friend?*

Inge's letters were filled with longings for home and concerns about my parents and me. She described how she waited for hours to get a phone call through to us but to no avail. She described watching the planes overhead, knowing they were on their way to bomb Braunschweig and that she "was scared." She described cold nights and snowy days and hoped that my mother and I would visit her on the official visiting day in the fall. In a letter dated September 29, 1944, she wrote that she was concerned about our house and wondered if repairs had been made after the bombing. She closed by writing, "With great longings and many thousands of greetings from my heart and millions of kisses, your loving Inge."

> "We scrambled out of the train and ran to hide in the field as a squadron of American P51 Mustangs swooped down to fire on the stopped train."

At the beginning of October 1944, my Mother and I did go to visit Inge. On the long trip, which required changing trains three times, the last train suddenly stopped and the conductor shouted, "All out, all out!" We scrambled out of the train and ran to hide in the field as a squadron of American P51 Mustangs swooped down to fire on the stopped train. As suddenly as they had appeared they left, and we shakenly climbed back on the train and continued our journey.

Mother and I spent 3 days with Inge, staying across the street from her school in a private home. For one night I was allowed to stay with my sister and five other girls who were her roommates. Although the bunk beds had straw mattresses, the water was cold, and there was no heat, it was an adventure for me and I had a wonderful time. With only one bathroom for all 18 girls and Frau Oppermann, we all had to wait in line. I spent an entire day with Inge and her classmates. On the third day my mother and I attended a play, one of the Grimm's fairy tales, performed by the students. On the fourth day we boarded the train for the return trip to Braunschweig. Happily it was an uneventful journey.

On the night of October 15, 1944, we all were asleep when once again the siren sounded. It was three o'clock in the morning and another bombing raid was underway. I put on my black gym suit and went down through the wine cellar to our family bunker with my parents leading the way. Our bunker had been built under a hill capped by three large beech trees. We had heard the planes before, but this time something was different. This time they were louder and the sound of the bombs lasted longer than ever before. My mother and father, Shura and another housemaid, and I huddled in terror in our small bunker as the bombardment went on and on. Because there was no electricity, the bunker was lit only by candles. There was nothing to do but to wait and pray and hope that it would be over soon. But it was not going to be over soon, not this time. We could not know the details, but overhead was a force of 233 four-engine British heavy bombers, each with a bomb load of approximately six tons. They had overflown Hanover and were now directly over Braunschweig. When the all-clear siren finally sounded, we climbed out of the bunker and up onto a nearby hill to see what was going on. Seeing the entire sky red and hearing the crashing and explosive sounds of buildings collapsing in the distance, I saw my parents cry for the first time.

That night more than 800 tons of bombs were dropped on the city of Braunschweig. A firestorm started in the wooden houses of the old town and spread quickly. The blast waves blew the roofs off houses and blew out windows. Hot masses of air were sucked upwards by the powerful thermal pressure that arose from the fire. It was strong enough to sweep small pieces of furniture into the air and toss people about. There followed a barrage of 200,000 phosphorus and incendiary bombs to spread the firestorm further. People tried to leave the inner city over the many bridges that crossed the Oker River, but many were trapped in the hot melting tar of the streets and burned to death.

> "Seeing the entire sky red and hearing the crashing and explosive sounds of buildings collapsing in the distance, I saw my parents cry for the first time."

Forty minutes after the first bombs were dropped, the raid was over but the firestorm burned for 2 ½ days. We would later learn it was started by the greatest bomb load dropped on any single day during World War II. Three German cities were firebombed resulting in great destruction and loss of life during the war: Dresden, Hamburg, and Braunschweig.

The fire brigade of Braunschweig made countless heroic rescues. In one case they freed 23,000 people who had been trapped in a bunker. Still, by the time the firestorm had been extinguished on October 17, more than 600 people had died and 80,000 were left homeless. My parents knew many who had lost everything and some who had lost their lives. Ninety percent of the Braunschweig city center had been destroyed.

My mother with Hans-Jürgen, 1945

CHAPTER FIVE

SURVIVAL

"So many of the prisoners, especially
the Russians, were on the loose, raiding
the homes of ordinary people and
stealing anything they wanted."

A year after the war's end

SOMEHOW, DESPITE THE BOMBING, OUR FAMILY HAD ACQUIRED SIX OR SEVEN CHICKENS AND A ROOSTER. They lived outside in a tree and my clever father had made a hole in the door of our large storage barn so the chickens could come inside to make nests and lay their eggs. One day my mother took me back to where one chicken was sitting on her eggs and said that it would not be long before the eggs hatched into little chicks. Then she told me that she too had an egg in her tummy and it would not be long before I had a little brother or a little sister. My mother was 39 years old; I think she was embarrassed to tell me that she was pregnant because people simply did not talk about things like that in those days, especially at her age. Nor did she ever mention that the baby was an "afterthought." I was thrilled to know I was going to have a little brother or baby sister.

By March 1945 the tide of war had changed. In battle after battle German troops were being defeated. Inge and the other children from Braunschweig who had been evacuated to the Hartz Mountains were told to pack up and prepare to leave. The enemy would soon reach their village. There was no transportation; they walked from their school to the train, carrying everything they owned. Many lugged suitcases full of jewelry, silver, and other items of value their parents had brought to them during their visits for safe keeping. In time, the road was littered with family treasures, too heavy for young children to carry.

We all were waiting for Inge when she arrived home. There was no great celebration, no party; only hugs and kisses to share the joy that we were together again. There were to be no more bombings because the German troops had fled the city, and we learned that the Americans were advancing very quickly toward Braunschweig. Hitler had told all German troops to "fight until you die," but most people knew the war was lost and preferred to surrender as an American prisoner of war than to be shot by a brown shirt or killed as part of a last stand for the Führer.

For 3 days and nights we heard gunfire from the city. One day a Nazi storm trooper came to our door to demand my mother accompany him to the bunker. Earlier she had refused to give them any more of her good china and the man was angry. "Come with me," he demanded. "No," she replied, "I'm a lady and when someone wants to talk to me that someone can come to me!" This was his second visit and still she was refusing to go with him to the bunker. She was a strong woman steeled by the war. I am very sure her stubborn ways saved her life. It was during those last three desperate days that the Nazis took 12 people known to be opposed to the Third Reich into the bunker and murdered them. One was the mayor of Braunschweig who after trying to commit suicide was taken away and shot.

Even after the German soldiers had retreated and the Americans were approaching the city we used our personal bunker because we felt safe there. I think it was April 10 or 11, 1945, just a few days after my 11th birthday, that we were in the bunker when we heard the sound of tanks. We had been in the bunker for 3 days listening to the distant shelling off and on and were eager to get out. We hoped they were American tanks. "Inge," my father said, "You go out, you speak English." Inge was just 13 and had only been studying English since she was 10, as was required in high school; but hesitant as she was, she went out with my father close behind. My mother and I followed. There, in front of us, stood six very dirty American soldiers. They asked if they could use our wash room and we said, "Yes, of course." Still they lined us up in front of our house, and one of them stood guard with a rifle. One by one, they went into the house and one by one they returned. The transformation was amazing! After they determined that we were harmless, they produced gifts. My father was given a cigar, my mother, a package of C-rations, and one of them gave Inge and me two long, flat, hard objects wrapped in silver paper and unlike anything we had ever seen before. We did not know what each one was or what we should do with it. Then, as we watched in curious amazement, the soldier unwrapped his stick of gum, put it into his mouth, and began

> "One day a Nazi storm trooper came to our door to demand my mother accompany him to the bunker."

to chew. We did the same; it was sweet and tasted very good. We chewed until our jaws hurt and every night, until it disappeared, we put our chewing gum back in its silver foil to rest by our night lamp until morning. I think one portion of gum lasted about 5 days. Now looking like rather normal human beings, the soldiers smiled and waved good-bye as they went on their way toward Berlin.

Not long after the soldiers left our house we were in the living room listening to the Grundig radio when a report came in from Berlin. The announcer said the allied troops were coming and this would likely be the last time that we would hear the German national anthem. As he played Haydn's "Deutschland, Deutschland, über Alles," we all had very strange, mixed feelings of happiness and sadness — happiness because the war was finally over and sadness that the Germany we knew would no longer exist but would lie in rubble, to be occupied by foreigners. The German high command did indeed sign an unconditional surrender on May 3, 1945. As the days wore on, news of the defeat of Germany filled the newspapers and the airwaves now in the control of the Allies. My father told us that Hitler and Eva Braun along with Joseph Göbbels and his wife had died from poisoning themselves and all six of the Göbbels' children. He also told us about the failed attempt by high-ranking German officers to assassinate Hitler and many other Germans during the war in an effort to stop the death and destruction. But that conclusion was not to be, and a vengeful Hitler had Claus von Stauffenberg and all the rest of them shot. Now, at last, the killing was finally over.

> "The announcer said the allied troops were coming and this would likely be the last time that we would hear the German national anthem."

During the war the greater Braunschweig region had become a vast Nazi slave labor center. Thousands of prisoners of war lived in the region in these camps and worked in the factories manufacturing the tools of war. Camps throughout the city housed slave laborers from Russia and Eastern Europe. When the Americans arrived many prisoners were set free to fend for themselves. No local police force existed, and the American MPs had their own work to do with the American soldiers. So many of the prisoners, especially the Russians, were on the loose, raiding the homes of ordinary people and stealing anything they wanted. They usually came to our house at dusk or later, when we were almost ready to go to bed. They would knock at the door and my father (still fluent in Russian) enlisted our Russian housemaid Shura for a unified defense. Because our home was also a restaurant, they always wanted schnapps. They stole a

We formed a line to pass bricks from our damaged school so they could be reused in reconstruction projects. I am standing third from the left.

variety of items from our home, including a typewriter on one occasion and a radio on another. We never tried to stop them for fear they would become violent. One of our friends told us the amusing story of how a Russian was trying to take the faucet from his wall. The Russian thought if he put it on his wall back home, he would have water. Recalling those post-war events, I do not believe I would be here today had it not been for my father's Russian and Shura's support.

With the end of the war, Shura wanted to go home to Russia and bring her mother back to work for and live with us in Germany forever. Even during the war, her life had been so much better with us than it had been in Russia. Back home she had been forced to join a railroad work crew to haul heavy railroad ties into place. So she went off to a location in town where the young Russian, Polish, and Czech women waited for transportation back to their homes. Just a week later she returned to us in tears. She told us how, every night, the American soldiers broke into their quarters and raped them. She had come to say good-bye before leaving for Russia. We never saw or heard from her again and believed, as with so many others who had worked in Germany during the war, she was shot as part of Stalin's program of vengeance.

One of the first signs of post-war normalcy in Braunschweig was the reopening of our school. Inge and I were excited to go back to our classes although half of the building had been destroyed. The school day was divided into three separate shifts: mornings for the older girls, afternoons for younger girls of my age, evenings for the boys whose school was in rubble.

In the spring of 1945, on June 10, my little brother Hans Jürgen was born in our home in the Nussberg. It was a wonderful, joyous day! My father was very proud to finally have a son; friends of the restaurant sent flowers, and we celebrated. Hans Jürgen was a very healthy boy who weighed nine and a half German pounds and measured 60 centimeters long. There was nothing to suggest he would not grow up to be a healthy child. But I am getting ahead of my story.

With an American soldier

CHAPTER SIX

THE AMERICAN OCCUPATION

"Lucky us, we found a soldier from Texas
who was happy to exchange a whole
carton of Lucky Strikes™ for a German
camera, even though it had no film in it."

With an American soldier

As the war was coming to an end and the combat troops had left, the American occupying force in Braunschweig arrived to put up a tented camp in the meadow near our restaurant. Judging from its large size it looked as if the Americans had come to stay. The meadow was full of jeeps and trucks, the camp was surrounded with barbed wire, and loud speakers played the first American music Inge and I had ever heard. I remember hearing Louis Armstrong and Ella Fitzgerald for the first time, along with someone singing "I Found My Thrill on Blueberry Hill." We tried to learn the lyrics and the music but when our father heard us practicing he quipped, "That's jungle music!" Then there was Glenn Miller's "In the Mood," which Inge and I quickly learned to play together on the piano. In those years, I had no way of knowing the effect that such music would have on me for the rest of my life. American Jazz would become my music. These days when I hear "In the Mood" or "I Found My Thrill on Blueberry Hill," I can still see that American tent city in the meadow near our home in the Nussberg.

From time to time American soldiers visited our restaurant. I remember one soldier in particular; he was the first black person we had ever seen. He had heard that there was a newborn baby in the restaurant, and he came every other day on his bike to bring us oranges. We took him upstairs to see my little brother and learned that he had a son back home whom he had never seen. I can still see his large black hand holding my brother's tiny white hand. He was very kind.

Throughout the war my enterprising father had hidden a few bottles of wine in the cellar and had built a small distillery to make schnapps. When some American soldiers asked if they could have a couple of bottles of schnapps, he offered to trade them for two army blankets. My mother had a friend who was a professional seamstress, and she turned the blankets into warm winter coats for Inge and me. We were happy and wore them with pride.

It was around that time, shortly after the end of the war, that my father took his two daughters to see a war exhibit in a museum in Braunschweig. We were horrified and wanted to leave. I was 12 and Inge was 15. The pictures revealed clear evidence of the Nazi concentration camps where so many had been tortured and murdered. My father had been right all along, although throughout the war none of us had any knowledge of the camps. The Party controlled all of the press and unless you lived next to one of those places or in a large city nearby, there was no way you could know. I remember being especially horrified when we were shown a lampshade made of human skin.

Most citizens of Braunschweig stayed away from the GI camp in the meadow, but not Inge and I. We were curious little girls and wandered over there often. My father knew about our visits, so he gave us a box camera that he had been hiding to trade for something useful. There was no film, just the camera. Inge and I walked through the camp and around the trucks and jeeps looking for someone who had something useful like cigarettes. On the black market cigarettes were very valuable, and my father could trade them for something we really needed, like food. Lucky us, we found a soldier from Texas who was happy to exchange a whole carton of Lucky Strikes™ for a German camera, even though it had no film in it. We made the exchange, and he made the mistake of leaving the camera on the seat of his jeep. Enterprising little girls that we were, we took it back and found another buyer who gave us a second carton of cigarettes. We never told our father just how enterprising we had been!

One warm day in the summer of 1945 we heard from one of our restaurant guests that General Eisenhower, the commander of the Allied forces in Europe, was coming to Braunschweig. No one mentioned that this famous American, who would one day become President of the United

> "One warm day in the summer of 1945 we heard from one of our restaurant guests that General Eisenhower, the commander of the Allied forces in Europe, was coming to Braunschweig. No one mentioned that this famous American, who would one day become President of the United States, was of direct German descent."

Inge and I in our Army blanket coats with Hans-Jürgen

States, was of direct German descent. We all went up on a hill overlooking the camp in the meadow and watched as Eisenhower arrived in a helicopter. Even from very far away we could see him disembark. It was impossible to get closer because the camp was surrounded by barbed wire and extra guards were on hand for this special occasion. However, we watched intently as Eisenhower greeted all of the high-ranking officers and then disappeared into one of the tents. About an hour later he came out, boarded the helicopter, and flew away.

The American camp in the meadow continued to function, and we became more and more adept at scavenging tobacco from the Americans' half-smoked cigarettes. We watched them sit on their helmets and smoke. Eventually there would be a large pile of butts next to the helmets and when no one was looking, we went to work. We collected every visible cigarette butt and took our

> "We took some of the fresh cigarettes that we had acquired through the camera exchange to the wounded German soldiers in the local hospital."

booty home, where we stripped the tobacco out of the paper and collected it in a can. It was great trading stuff! We took some of the fresh cigarettes that we had acquired through the camera exchange to the wounded German soldiers in the local hospital. I can still remember being in the hospital hallway and seeing a soldier who had lost both of his legs. He pushed himself along on a board with wheels.

My father was pleased with the results of our tobacco hunt; he took our jar out to the black market to trade for butter, or apples, or whatever he could get. Sometimes he would come home with a sausage and we would have a big feast. We were happy to have made a contribution to the family's constant hunt for food.

After 3 months or so, the Americans left and the meadow was empty. Some fortunate local families like ours were allowed to dig up a small plot of earth to grow food. I remember we had our own garden of potatoes, carrots, red beets, and beans. We also kept rabbits, and Inge and I collected grass for them to eat. On holidays we would cook a chicken or a rabbit for dinner, and that meal was very special.

After the Americans had gone east to Berlin and the French had occupied the Rhineland, the British came to occupy Braunschweig. They were as hungry as we and came to the restaurant often. At least once a week, their officers used the restaurant as a gathering place where they brought their own food and often shared it with us. It was like Christmas. Inge and I would sing and play the piano, and they would give us some of their delicious desserts. Then they taught us this crazy dance they called the "Hokey Pokey." I remember that they were very nice, and a few years later one of their higher ranking officers came back to visit.

Even after the Americans were gone, our high school continued to serve a daily ration of soup from big soup kettles. We started a pen pal program with an American school in a place called "Seattle," and as part of the program we received two care packages. I remember the arrival of the first package, which contained two dresses, one for Inge and one for me. I could not participate in the pen pal program because I had just started to study English and did not know enough to write, but Inge did.

From the end of the war in 1945 through 1948, food became less and less available. My mother did the best she could, making soup from tree bark and cooking a few vegetables from our little garden. She often used sawdust as filler. As I have mentioned, on holidays there was an occasional chicken or rabbit but no milk — nothing to nourish a growing boy like my little brother.

For the next 3 years, from 1945 until we were rescued by the American Marshall Plan in 1948, hunger was a way of life. During these years, my father and I would occasionally go to the railway station hoping to find space on a train to the village of Grosshimstedt, where my father was born and where his two brothers, Herman and Gustav, still lived. The trains were packed and even when we could get aboard, the ride was long and uncomfortable. Our train would stop at a river where we had to disembark and wade across the water to wait for another train, whenever it would come.

I remember our first visit to Grosshimstedt. When we finally got off the train, we walked along a road some distance before we reached the village. My uncles and aunts were of course glad to know we had survived the bombing, and they welcomed us into their homes. They also knew we had come to beg for food. They shared what they could, and my uncles directed my father to people who would look at some of our personal belongings such as the jewelry or clothes we had outgrown and had brought along to exchange for fresh food or canned goods or sometimes bacon. We made the long trip to Grosshimstedt often during those hungry years. Back in Braunschweig when we found that a bakery had some bread for sale, one of us would stand in line for hours. Inge tells the story of having stood in line for a long time and just as she was to enter the store, the baker announcing "No more bread!" Sadly, she had to come home empty handed that day.

"We started a pen pal program with an American school in a place called 'Seattle,' and as part of the program we received two care packages."

Things were a little better at our school. The American troops had donated large barrels of soup for the children. We brought our own bowls and utensils and shared the "soup of the day" — lentil, potato, or pea. Our favorite was a sweet soup. I remember the women of the city coming to our school and forming long lines to move the bricks away from the destroyed building. The students' job was to pile up the bricks so that they could be reused in the reconstruction of other city buildings.

One day my father came home with what I remember as the second big package that had come from Seattle as part of our pen pal program. This time the box contained clothing and food; we were overjoyed! We did not care that the sweaters had holes in the elbows or the shoes were worn through. Once again, it was like Christmas.

As time passed, Hans Jürgen became very sick, a victim of malnutrition. Perhaps because my mother carried him through the last year of the war, when we were confined to our bunker, his chances of becoming a healthy child were reduced, but now his nutritional status had become desperate. My mother gave him many direct blood transfusions, which Dr. Konoopka supervised in our home; but even those emergency measures did not help, and my parents finally took him to the hospital. The doctor said that to continue the medication he had prescribed would cause damage to Hans Jürgen's equilibrium and affect other organs, so our parents stopped the medicine and prayed for a miracle.

> "As time passed, Hans Jürgen became very sick, a victim of malnutrition. Perhaps because my mother carried him through the last year of the war, when we were confined to our bunker, his chances of becoming a healthy child were reduced, but now his nutritional status had become desperate."

Throughout the fall and winter of 1950, my little brother's condition grew worse and worse until December 18, a date I remember vividly. I was in my classroom when the principal came in and asked me to come out into the hall. Standing there together, he told me that my little brother had become very sick and I should go home right away. I ran out of the school and all the way home as fast as I could, but when I arrived, he had already died. We all were in tears. It was the saddest day in my young life.

Just a few days before Christmas, Dr. Henneberger, the clergyman who had baptized my brother, came to conduct the funeral. Dr. Henneberger was a good friend of my parents and a frequent guest in our restaurant. Following the traditional German service, Hans Jürgen was buried in the children's section of the Braunschweig city cemetery, the "Hauptfriedhof." He was just 5 ½ years old.

And then it was Christmas. We tried very hard not to cry when we saw the used tricycle that my father had somehow found to give his little son. All of these years later, I still remember that Christmas of 1950 and all of us singing "Stille Nacht" with tears in our eyes. It was the worst Christmas ever.

My best high school friends.

CHAPTER SEVEN

PUTTING LIFE BACK TOGETHER

"My parents had survived the war as well as the death of their young son, and they were doing their very best to put their lives and ours back together again."

Dancing lessons, 1950

I HAVE OFTEN WONDERED WHAT IT WOULD HAVE BEEN LIKE IF MY LITTLE BROTHER HAD LIVED. Inge and I were young girls growing up in a new post-war world, yet memories of the recent past were always with us. Somehow, things were different now. Even as an adult, I cannot imagine my parents' sorrow. I know the loss of such a young child was an unbelievable tragedy. He is still missed today, and for Inge and me the hurt of losing our little brother has never gone away. Nevertheless, life did go on and when I was 16, I was allowed to begin dancing lessons at Tanz Schule Heussler. Actually the instruction at this well-known school included etiquette as well as ballroom dancing — all part of growing up in Germany, part of one's social education. My class of girls was joined by a class of boys, and I must say that we girls seemed to learn much faster than the boys! We learned every dance in the book, including the rumba, the quick step, the tango, and of course the waltz. I enjoyed the classes and was a good dancer. What I learned back then would be with me the rest of my life; I am told that I am still a good dancer.

In Germany students in the mid-1900s entered high school at age 10 and immediately began to study English. At 13 they had to choose between Latin and French (I chose

French) in addition to English, of course. At 17 they could choose a third language, and I would choose Spanish. For me all these languages would come in very handy later on, but I am getting ahead of my story.

I enjoyed school and was a good student. I took a full schedule of 16 subjects per week, including 2 hours of sport, 1 hour of music, and 1 hour of religion. I loved geography, history, and music as I still do. Both my music and French teachers were men, and they were the best. We always stood up when the teacher came into the class; it was the rule. Most of our classes were held in the same room, where students shared tables and benches, three to a bench. Because there were no lockers, we had to keep all of our books under our bench. We wrote with pens that we dipped into an inkwell. Anyone who misbehaved had to stand in the corner, which I remember doing once when Frau Althaus said I should not have been talking.

Before the war boys and girls attended separate schools, but our city fathers decided to take advantage of the building that once housed the German paratroopers to create a new co-educational facility, "The Wilhelm Raabe Gymnasium." It was a first in all of Lower Saxony. Because the school was near our house and offered small classes, I was happy to change schools. Only 14 boys and six girls were in my class, and the boys and girls were in constant competition. In the old school there had been 42 girls in a single classroom.

This new school building also held a small studio theater where I saw my first plays, both American: "Our Town" by Thornton Wilder and "The Glass Menagerie" by Tennessee Williams. I got to know the actors because they came to our restaurant, and I was enthralled by a young man named Hans-Jörg Felmy, who went on to become

My class at Lyzeum Kleine Burg, 1949

An early theater production (second young man from the left is Hans-Jörg Felmy who went on to star in many movies)

a very well-known stage and film star. One of his movies was "The Prize," about the Nobel Prize, starring Julie Andrews and Paul Newman. These experiences launched my life-long interest in the theater.

My parents had survived the war as well as the death of their young son, and they were doing their very best to put their lives and ours back together again. They worked hard to make the restaurant as successful as it had been before the bombing, and they needed Inge and me to help. It was, after all, a family business. Every day after school and every evening we worked in the restaurant. I loved the contact with people, and although we had many waiters, I would often help serve by pouring the beer and cider and placing it on the waiters' trays. We gave tokens to the waiters who used them to pay for drinks from the bar and food from the kitchen. When a customer paid his waiter, the waiter would keep the money until all of the guests had left and he would then settle up at the end of the evening, when he would pay us for his tokens and keep what was left as his tip. It is a system still used in some of the German beer halls today.

Our father was a man of strict discipline. If he saw us doing our school work while working in the restaurant, he would say, "Don't you have anything better to do? Go help your mother in the kitchen." Sometimes Inge and I had to scrub the outside tables and chairs and iron the many tablecloths. When my mother needed milk, we would

The "King of the Nussberg" with his staff

Our head waiter, Heinz Engel

ride our bikes to the nearby village of Riddagshausen and return with the cans full of milk balanced on our handlebars. Although the ride to Riddagshausen was downhill, the return trip home was uphill and was very hard work.

I still remember seeing large barrels of beer delivered to our restaurant by horse-drawn wagons. The men who brought the beer wore leather aprons, unloaded the barrels from the horse wagon, and rolled them to where they were dropped down into our cellar. Three hoses ran from the barrels up into the bar where they were attached to three faucets, one for dark beer and two for light. Somehow my father always knew when the beer was ready to run out and went to the basement to reposition the hoses in the new barrels.

Once again the Restaurant Nussberg was a busy place. When the weather was good and there were many guests, usually on the weekends, we had an orchestra. Guests regularly

Students at our
restaurant

came to play the popular
German card game "Skat,"
and once a week a men's choir
came from the nearby village
of Riddagshausen to sing
and have dinner. Often there
were hundreds of guests in
the outdoor garden, and Inge
and I would wash, dry, and
refill glasses all evening long. I
also kept track of the waiters'
tokens. I still remember those
nights as Inge and I watched
couples dancing in the open
air. We were both so busy that

Back to normal

my mother prepared a plate of food for us so that we could eat
and work, enjoy the music, and watch the dancing. A new era
was beginning and once again, I am happy to recall, my father
was "the King of the Nussberg."

"King of the Nussberg" at war's end

CHAPTER EIGHT

ADVENTURES IN A POST-WAR WORLD

"I was a teenager on the loose, but I did
have my parents blessing…. They had said,
'Well, if you can afford it, go.' So go we did,
but affording it was another matter."

Tenting on the beach

THE WORLD WAS SAFE AGAIN, THERE WAS FOOD TO EAT, AND I WAS
LOOKING FOR ADVENTURE. It was the spring of 1950, and we were on vacation
from school. Two of my girlfriends, Martina Müller-Hofstede and Lilo Prehn, and I set
off on our bicycles for a trip north to Lutjenburg, a land of spas and resorts and a beach
– valuable resources not available in Braunschweig. Lutjenburg was 140 miles away!

I was a teenager on the loose, but I did have my parents' blessing to take some time
off from my work at the restaurant. They had said, "Well, if you can afford it, go."
So go we did, although affording it was another matter. It was a new experience for
everyone: three bikes, one tent, one cook stove, and a meager supply of food. Our first
stop was a youth hostel where we arrived late and, exhausted, fell asleep immediately.

We pedalled all the next day and finally reached the sea. It was hilly and from time
to time we had to get off our bikes and walk, although even walking was difficult.
While we were putting our tent up in a pouring rainstorm, passersby were laughing
their heads off. Our tent looked more like a device for collecting water. We clearly did
not know what we were doing; none of us had ever put up a tent before. Inside our
canvas shelter we had brought some straw and a blanket for each of us. We had very
little money, and on the second day our portable cook stove exploded. So much for
home cooking!

The next day we met a butcher who sold hearty soups full of potatoes and meat.

Having had no breakfast, we decided to spend some of the little money we had for lunch at his shop. He must have felt sorry for us because he gave us a little more than we actually paid for. From our new butcher friend we learned that every 3 days in this resort town there was an amateur "Jekami" event ("Jeder Kann Mitmachen" translated literally means "everyone can participate") with singing, dancing, painting, and you name it. Wandering around town we came across posters that announced, "Any person who participates in the Jekami will get a free dinner." Of course we were ready to do whatever was necessary for a free dinner.

We drew straws to determine in which order we would perform. Martina would be first and would sing, I would be second and would play "In the Mood" on the piano (I think I also sang), and Lilo would be third although I do not remember what she did. In any event, we all got our free dinners.

At the end of our 10 days in this beach resort town it was time to go home. Lilo went on along the sea with two other school friends, and Martina and I rode our bikes to the next town where we put them on the train so we could hitchhike home. We were tired of pedaling. I know it sounds crazy, but everyone hitchhiked in those days even though there were very few cars. Martina, who was near sighted, had a little monkey puppet that she waved at the cars going by, and the drivers must have thought she was nuts because she was trying to wave down cars that were full of people. I finally hailed a Volkswagen with only two people in it, both of whom turned out to be sportswriters who lived in Hamburg and worked for the newspaper there. They asked whether we were afraid, two young girls out on the road alone, which prompted Martina to answer, "No, we have a weapon to defend ourselves" – and she pulled a large kitchen knife out of her bag!

I told them I had a brother in Hamburg, which was not true of course. I did, however, have a friend — Rolf Gartz — who studied architecture in Braunschweig and whose parents lived in Hamburg. Soon, the two sportswriters dropped us off in front of the house I knew to be that of Rolf's parents, and as they drove off, I rang the doorbell. When the door opened, there stood a woman I had never seen before — a complete stranger. Undaunted, I introduced myself as a friend of her son, and she graciously remarked, "If you're looking for a place to stay you can sleep here on the couches" — which we did! The next morning the Volkswagen returned, and one of the reporters took us back to the highway and let us out.

Before long we hailed down a large car with a Dutch license plate. The driver stopped some distance ahead, and we ran to ask him for a ride. He asked if we knew the way to Hanover and we said, "Yes, we do" although in truth we did not. We had never been to Hanover. The driver turned out to be a carpet merchant, and somehow we managed to lead him into the inner city of Hanover. He invited us to join him at a very famous coffee house, "Café Kröpke," where we sat outside and enjoyed the beautiful day. When our new friend then called for a cake, a waitress appeared with a cart full of beautiful cakes, and we stuffed ourselves! The carpet merchant smiled when he saw how hungry we were. Knowing that we had no money, he took us all the way back to the autobahn.

Thus our adventure continued: two sportswriters, an unknown woman, and a carpet merchant. Who would be next? We hailed another Volkswagen, a green one this time, and the driver was a candy salesman traveling alone to Berlin. The seats were covered with boxes of candy that he moved aside so we would have a place to sit. "Help yourself!" he insisted, and he took us all the way to Braunschweig and let us out at the edge of the city.

For the last leg of our trip we hailed down a tiny three-wheeled truck loaded with vegetables. Somehow we managed to find a place to sit behind the driver as part of the cargo on the open platform. The man was a farmer and he took us all the way home to the Nussberg. My parents were glad to see me, but I did get a lecture on how irresponsible we had been to hitchhike all the way home from the sea. We thought it was an adventure! Inge had made the same trip earlier and whatever my sister did, I had to do too.

While I was away Inge had been working for an electrical company in Braunschweig. At the end of the first month she was proud and happy to come home with her first paycheck, until she sensed that our father was not happy. "Where's your paycheck?" he asked. Inge was shocked. She had done the work, and she assumed the pay was hers. Apparently my father saw things differently: "You live here and you eat here. If you don't want to pay for that, you can move out." Inge was no longer happy; she gave him her paycheck and he gave her five marks in return. She did not move out, not yet.

I was very happy in my studies at the Wilhelm Raabe Schule. I was having fun and learning a lot in the much smaller classes compared with my previous school, and I thought the teachers were

My class at the Wilhelm Raabe Gymnasium, 1951

great. I also got to know some of the boys in the higher classes and found out that they liked jazz as much as I did. One day a boy named Ulrich Everling, who became a life-long friend, mentioned that a group of them would be driving to Hamburg to hear "Jazz at the Philharmonic," and he invited me to go along. I was thrilled and of course said "yes" even before asking my parents.

I did not know it then, but back in 1945 an American record producer named Norman Grantz had signed contracts with every major jazz performer in the United States to make recordings and play in live concerts under the banner of "Jazz at the Philharmonic". They were the best of the best, and I was going to hear some of them live in Hamburg! Among the artists were Ella Fitzgerald, Oscar Peterson, and Gene Krupa. Granz's musicians first toured the United States in 1945. In 1951 the group was on a European tour that opened in Copenhagen and would go on to every major European city including Hamburg. I could not wait; jazz had become part of my life. My parents could not understand the attraction, why would I want to drive all the way to Hamburg and back in a tiny car to hear that "jungle music?" But I was going to hear some of the greatest jazz musicians in the world, and I did not care what they thought.

It was a long 3-hour drive to Hamburg in what I remember was a very small car. There were five of us, four boys and I, and it was February 26, 1951. Before we left my friend Rolf Hamster, whose father owned a record and radio shop in Braunschweig and was a friend of my parents, gave me two pictures and said, "Please get autographs from Ella Fitzgerald and Oscar Peterson." I had learned that the famous drummer Gene Krupa would also be playing as would bassist Ray Brown. Of the two performances we chose to go only to the matinee so we could drive home in the early evening. Of course we bought the cheapest seats, but still the concert was the best and I was there!

I had Rolf Hamster's pictures with me, and at the end of the concert I was determined to do what I had promised, to get those autographs. I headed for the stage but was stopped by a guard. "Where do you think you're going?" he demanded, to which I replied, "I left my glove in the

Mission accomplished: autographed pictures of Ella and Oscar

aisle and I need to find it." There was no glove, of course, but I was not going to miss my chance to get those autographs. When the guard turned his head, I darted up on the stage and there they were, Ella and Oscar. I was very polite and asked if they would please sign my photographs. They said, "Of course," and all I can remember today was that they were very nice and very friendly, and that I was very pleased and proud to have accomplished my mission. Even today when I am asked to approach perfect strangers to sell tickets to our Traverse Symphony raffle or a Rotary event, I say, "It's easy to ask, they can only say yes or no." Fortunately Ella and Oscar said "yes!"

The concert had been fabulous, and the boys and I were on cloud nine. Afterward, anyone who could afford a disc bought one, but I had used up my money to buy my ticket. In later years I would buy lots of discs and see Ella Fitzgerald three more times. She is still the best and my favorite jazz singer. We drove home right after the matinee and I could not wait to present the autographed photos to Rolf Hamster, who immediately posted them in his store window. I so wish I had them today. Then it was back to reality. For the next 6 months I went to school, took piano lessons, attended dance classes and of course worked every evening for my father in the restaurant.

In September of 1951, when I was 17, we had a school exchange sponsored by the Worldwide Friendship Organization. My class of girls went to Copenhagen where I stayed with the

School Exchange of World Friendship Association in Copenhagen

In Copenhagen

Tove

family of a girl my age named Tove Bang. Tove and I had a wonderful time together. We went to a jazz club in Hellerup, a suburb of Copenhagen, and we visited two breweries. We played tennis, bicycled a lot, visited many museums, attended a beautiful ballet at the Royal Theater, and went to the Kronberg Castle. I kissed my first boy in Copenhagen; or did he kiss me?

A year later, as part of the exchange, Tove came to Braunschweig where we had lots of fun together and enjoyed going to the first ice cream parlor in Braunschweig where all of the young people "hung out." Tove and I corresponded for many years; she married a Frenchman and we lost contact.

As I have related, after the war there was a shortage of everything, which persisted

Standing proud in our new dresses

The 1951 Braunschweig Police Variety Show

into the 1950s. My mother asked our wonderful seamstress, Mrs. Karges, who had made our coats from the US Army blankets, to create two new white dresses for Inge and me from tablecloths. We were thrilled: two very stylish new dresses! Our mother was so clever. Which reminds me of the time when Inge's dancing class was holding their final formal dance where the boys were to wear suits and the girls, long dresses. But Inge had no long dress until my mother came to the rescue. She used white curtains from the bedroom, some cloth flowers from her hat, and a lavender sash to make a beautiful long dress. Inge's date, Helmut Giesecke, was astounded at how beautiful she looked.

Four hands: "In the Mood"

As normal life gradually returned, the Braunschweig police department once again put on their annual "show." In 1951 they asked Inge and me to participate, and we were pleased when my dad agreed that we could accept. We played the piano, four hands: "In the Mood" of course.

These were the best of years. Braunschweig was known not only for its fine architectural university but also as the home of the most famous milling school in Europe – the same school where my father had studied in the late 1920s. Now in the 1950s students came from all over the world. I recall two milling students from Argentina because one night they were up on the roof of our ballroom celebrating and making a lot of noise. Their parents had emigrated to Argentina from Germany, and the family was very wealthy. The boys shouted down, "Free beer for everyone!" When my father asked, "Why the celebration?" they replied, "Eva Peron has died, let's celebrate!" Their families had lost a great deal under the Peron dictatorship so they were happy that she was dead and the Peronist era had ended.

Inge and I continued to work at the restaurant. Things were better now. A real truck brought the beer. There were big crowds and music more and more frequently. Yes, there was a lot of work during those years, but there also was a lot of fun. Inge and I were not allowed to travel during the busy summer months; but when things slowed down in the spring and the fall, and we had saved what little money we had, we were off. My parents gave us money for railway tickets, but we used it for other things because we hitchhiked everywhere. Whenever we had a night off from the restaurant we attended events at the university, went out with students, and listened to as much live jazz as we could. We were both "hooked" on American jazz.

During spring vacation in 1952 Inge and I were off to Amsterdam, where we went to jazz clubs, saw movies, and toured the city via the many waterways. We were invited to stay with the family of a milling student Frans de Smet, a friend we knew in Braunschweig who was home for spring break. We stayed with the wonderful de Smet family and their seven children for several days and then went on to the historic city of Volendam, where all of the buildings looked old and people still wore wooden shoes. We toured the island of Marken, which was

Inge and I with Franz de Smet, our host in Holland

Me

Inge

even more historic than Volendam; visited the spa city of Scheveningen and Den Haag, which used to be the capital of the Netherlands; and took a train to Rotterdam, then the largest harbor in northern Europe that had been almost totally destroyed by German bombers.

After our wonderful time together in Holland, we had to think about going home. We met a man who said he was going to Trier, and that was good enough for us; we could easily hitchhike from Trier to Braunschweig. The man was a wine merchant whose car was filled with wine. We made numerous stops at restaurants along the way so he and his customer could sample his wines. We never did figure out how he could drink all that wine and not get tipsy, but he appeared to succeed. He drove us all the way to Trier, where as you know we had lived before the war when we were little girls. We stayed in a youth hostel overnight and hitched back to Braunschweig in the morning.

In Holland

When I reached the legal age of 18, I could apply for a driver's license, but first I had to learn how to drive. I took lessons at a commercial driving school and passed with flying colors, although I recall that shifting was very "complicated."

Our bus trip through Europe

Paris: Montmartre

Then on October 5, 1953 (I know the date only because Inge and I both kept simple diaries and made daily notes about our exploits), Inge had a vacation from her job and we signed up together for a student tour of five European countries: Holland, Belgium, France, Switzerland, and Italy. It was going to be a long trip, but we were eager to get out of Braunschweig. The tour company carried tents in a trailer behind the bus and set them up in cities like Paris, which was the most wonderful city of all. We went up to Montmartre, met two young boys, and danced in the street to the French "bal musette" music.

From Paris the bus took us south to Avignon and to Cavalière on the Côte d'Azure, where we pitched our tent and got caught in the rain. At the Grand Hotel Moriaz we noticed that a ping-pong tournament was in progress and the boys who were playing asked if we wanted to play. We did, and I was the big winner, having always played quite well. Years earlier I had belonged to a ping-pong club, and I was the second best youth player in Lower Saxony.

It was also at the Grand Hotel Moriaz in Cavalière that I met a young man named George who was vacationing with his family from Lyon. He mentioned that his aunt was looking for an au pair girl to teach their young son German. It was not until a year later that I would follow up on the connection, which would lead to a job in Lyon with the family of young Michel Mathieu. But once again, I am getting ahead of my story.

From southern France our bus took us on to Milan, Padua, and Lago Maggiore, where we boarded a steamship that took us to the island of Isola Bella. Inge and I went to an Italian restaurant and ordered our first spaghetti ever. I still remember the horrified reaction of our waiter as he watched us cut the noodles with our knives and forks. We quickly learned this was "not acceptable!" From Lago Maggiore we drove through Switzerland making several interesting stops before arriving home in Braunschweig. This unforgettable journey made us realize that there was much more of the world to see, and much more to learn.

With George in Cavalière

In Switzerland

In Marseille

The three Fasterding women

CHAPTER NINE

MY HIGH-FLYING SISTER

"That night Inge took me to a famous Frankfurt jazz club she knew about called the 'Domicile du Jazz.'"

Dick Visnak introduced Inge to the Pan Am representative.

BETWEEN THE TWO WORLD WARS, GERMANY HAD BEEN A PIONEER IN THE DEVELOPMENT OF COMMERCIAL AVIATION. Until the Hindenburg disaster in 1937, German airships had amazed the world. The first German airline, "Deutsche Luft Hansa," was created in 1926, providing commercial service until the start of the war, when it was taken over by the National Socialists and operated as they directed throughout the war. With the end of World War II in 1945, the company was dissolved as directed by the Allies.

Now, in 1953, a new company by the name of "Lufthansa" was created, and commercial aviation was to become part of the post-war German economy. At that time only three airlines were operating in Germany – Pan American Airlines (Pan Am), Air France, and British Overseas Airways Corporation (BOAC). Although Inge knew that her prospects were slim, she was determined. And if Inge was determined, so was I! I said, "Let's go to Frankfurt and get you an interview with Pan Am."

First we persuaded our butcher's son, Willi Meyer, to drive us to Frankfurt. We began by looking for the Chief Stewardess for Pan Am at the Frankfurt airport: no luck. Willi had gone on to visit friends and we were on our own. "Well," I said, "we're in Frankfurt, let's go to the American Forces radio station and look up that disc jockey we listen to all the time." So we took a bus and then a street car and found our way to the radio station a few miles outside Frankfurt in Hoest. We went up to the guard house and were confronted by a military policeman (MP) in white spats and a helmet. The station was located in a beautiful building that likely belonged to some person of royalty, a duke or an earl, before the war. And there we stood looking at the impressive building from across the street and Inge said, "And now what?" So I went across the street to the MP and said, "I have an interview with the host of "The Duffle Bag," which was the name of the radio show we listened to at home. I had no appointment of course, but that did not stop me from saying that I did. During the war we had learned not only to be independent but also to be a little aggressive; I had learned my lessons well. The MP asked, "Where are you from?" to which I answered, "The British Zone – I'm working for the Braunschweiger Zeitung" (the city newspaper in Braunschweig). I waved to Inge to come over, and the MP called another soldier who took us inside the building and into a room with a large glass window. There spinning records in the studio was my interview subject, Dick Visnak. Our guide said that the disc jockey would be finished in 10 minutes and that we should wait.

When Mr. Visnak came out I introduced myself and Inge. I told him the same story that I had told the MP and he said, "Okay, let's go to the canteen and have some lunch so we can talk." Well, we did and I must have felt guilty because I immediately confessed that I did not work for the Braunschweiger Zeitung but that the interview was for my school newspaper. I further confessed that the real reason we came to Frankfurt was not to see him but to find the head stewardess for Pan Am because Inge was looking for a job. We were stunned when he stood up and spoke to a woman at the next table who, amazingly, turned out to be just the right person at the right time. She was very pleasant and said she would arrange an appointment for us to talk to the appropriate Pan Am person the very next day. I did, by the way, interview Dick Visnak. He was a GI who had been a disk jockey in the states and was very happy doing whatever he was doing in Germany. We stayed overnight at a private home in Frankfurt with rented rooms, and the next morning Inge had her interview…but not a job.

That night Inge took me to a famous Frankfurt jazz club she knew about called the "Domicile du Jazz" ("the home of jazz"). The club was located in the basement of a bombed-out house and attracted the best jazz musicians in Germany. It was wonderful! In the years ahead I would return there often to develop many life-long friendships and one night to meet a handsome American soldier. But yes, once again I am getting ahead of my story.

Willi drove us home the next day, and we told our parents that Inge had a job as a stewardess, which of course she did not – not yet. They were very disappointed that she would be leaving home. Then on April 13, 1953, it was official; she was indeed offered a position as stewardess at Pan American Airlines and would begin immediately. It was the job that would change her life – and mine too, in so many ways. As I continue to say, whatever my sister did, I wanted to do too.

CHAPTER TEN

CLUB MARLIS

"Those two seasons of Club Marlis
were absolutely wonderful."

Inge and I at the Domicile du Jazz in Frankfurt, the place that inspired me to create "Club Marlis."

INGE AND I AND ALL OF OUR FRIENDS HAD COME TO LOVE AMERICAN MUSIC, ESPECIALLY JAZZ. In my new school for boys and girls, the first of its kind in our area of Lower Saxony, many of the boys who played instruments and played together in a band also loved the American music. One day in late fall or winter someone said, "Why don't we get together and play at the restaurant in the Nussberg?" When I then went to my father and asked if we might convert our former ballroom into a "jazz club," he greatly surprised me by saying, "Okay, but don't ask for a penny from me, and remember we need the space for our guests in the spring!"

We were thrilled although we knew there would be lots of hard work ahead if we were going to pull this off. We first began thinking about how to convert the large open space into a more intimate "club." Taking inspiration from the Domicile du Jazz in Frankfurt, we began by getting some long bamboo poles and fabric to lower the ceiling and make the place feel more "intimate." We found some large beer barrels to serve as tables, and put straw covers over the wall sconces so they would look like Italian wine bottles. We took the curtains down and blocked the windows with sheets of old plywood, which we painted black. One of the people from our local theater who was very

Curby Alexander and Bill Coleman

Eddie de Haas

interested in coming to the jazz club painted caricatures of musicians in white on the black panels.

I went to the local liquor distributor and offered to use their products if they would give us one of the bar sections with high chairs that they used at fairs. I guess I was persuasive because the man said "yes." Thus, we had a corner bar complete with stools. Probably the most ingenious thing we did was to go to the German railroad and ask if they had any of the old wooden benches with high backs that they could spare. They too said "yes," so we immediately had seating for forty or fifty jazz fans. "Club Marlis" was almost a reality.

This project was truly a cooperative effort among friends. The four boys who were really helpful — Rolf Hamster, Uli Everling, Horst Windhausen, and Klaus Franke — are still good friends and still jazz fans. At last Club Marlis was ready to open; it looked and sounded like a real jazz club! We soon added a "club card" and a charge of 2 marks a month. We changed the color of the card every month, and someone was always at the door to check people in. We wanted to be an exclusive club for upper class students and for our friends from the theater. Many people in the area were part of the black market, and we certainly did not want them in our club.

When my father saw how successful we were and how many people came and paid to get in, he jokingly asked, "Well, where's my money? I didn't charge you rent." He could not believe how many people came to listen to "that" music, and he never did charge us rent. We closed down in the spring of 1954 because my parents needed the space for the restaurant. However, Dad allowed us to put it back up in the fall for a second year, when we began to attract professional musicians who were willing to come by for a "one-night stand."

A number of music clubs called "Tabu" were in business in Germany in the 1950s, and they were owned by the parents of Romy Schneider, the actress who starred in the "Sisi" movies. The Tabu club in Braunschweig was located in an old bunker. When we went there and asked some of the musicians if they could come and play in Club Marlis, many of them agreed although they were surprised there was a jazz club that was run by students. When a jazz group from

France was playing one night at our local theater, my friends and I went to visit. After they finished playing I asked if they would come and play in our jazz club and they had responded, "What jazz club?", I told them about Club Marlis. I was developing a pretty good sales pitch. Ultimately they said, "Sure" they would come, and I was delighted. When I asked, "How much do I have to pay you?", they laughed and said, "If we can eat and drink as much as we want… you don't have to pay us anything."

So it was that I met my life-long friend, bassist Eddie de Haas who lived in Paris and played with Bill Coleman's big band. Years later, when I moved to Chicago, I looked him up and we have stayed in touch ever since. We still call each other to reminisce on our birthdays.

We advertised the addition of live, professional musicians like crazy, without spending any money of course, and that first "live" night we had more than one hundred guests

Sensationsgastspiel

BILL COLEMAN

and his Negros Swing Stars

DAS EREIGNIS FÜR HAMBURG!

Täglich 20 Uhr · Sonnabends 19 Uhr · Sonntags 17 Uhr

BILL COLEMAN

gilt nach Louis Armstrong als einer der besten Trompeter der Welt. Er hat eine großartige Karriere gemacht. Seine mehr als 150 Schallplattentitel erfreuen sich in der ganzen Welt großer Beliebtheit.

Curby Alexander, Alt-Saxophon und Clarinette

Zu den bekannten Orchestern, in denen er als Solist mitwirkte, zählen: Claude Hopkins, Hot-Lips-Page, Roy Eldrigde, Cat Anderson, Eddie Wilcox, Lucky Millinder.

Wallace Bishop, der beste Drummer in Europa

früher Solist von Earl Hines, Sy Oliver und Louis Armstrong. Sein musikalisches Gehör und sein unwahrscheinliches Tempo sichert dem Orchester den großen Erfolg.

Eddie O'Hare, Schlagbaß

Geboren am 21. Februar 1930 in Java-Bandung, ein ausgezeichneter Nachwuchskünstler, der exclusiv bei Bill Coleman verpflichtet ist. Sein turbulentes Spiel löst größte Begeisterung aus.

Herman Wilson, Posaune

Ein hervorragender Könner, der sich als Solist in bekannten Orchestern einen Namen gemacht hat.

Jack Starling, Jazzpianist

Dieser französische Jazzpianist mit brillanter Technik vertritt die Linie von George Shearing.

Cecily Forde, Neger-Jazzsängerin Nr. 1

Diese charmante Künstlerin kommt aus Trinidad und versteht es, durch ihre rassige, aber sehr melodische Art, das Publikum zu begeistern.

altona 10872 2000 2 55

including our friends from the theater who came over after their performance. Everyone cheered and the musicians ate and drank and played until 2:00 in the morning. They especially loved our "Riesenbockwurst" because it looked like an American foot-long hot dog. My father complained that we all were up too late having too much fun. He would never be a jazz fan and he just did not understand. Regrettably, Inge missed all of the fun because she was off on her own adventure as a stewardess for Pan Am.

There was another success at Club Marlis that would stay with me for the rest of my life. The American troops based in Helmstedt on the border of East and West Germany had a pretty boring life listening to music on the Russian radio, so on the weekends, when they would come to Braunschweig, and somehow found Club Marlis. They loved to dance, were happy to teach us, and did we dance! The "jitterbug" was our favorite, but they taught us lots of other steps too. I have loved to dance ever since, and I still thank the GIs from Helmstedt for those early lessons. On Thursdays we continued to use recordings, but on Friday and Saturday we were "live," even though the musicians were usually students from my school. Every now and then some British soldiers would bring their instruments to the club and jam well into the night.

Those two seasons of Club Marlis were absolutely wonderful! I kept busy working in my parents' restaurant during the day and in the jazz club at night. When the club closed down at the end of 1954, I decided to pursue the job that George had suggested a year before – the au pair position with the Mathieu family in Lyon, France. Yet another adventure was on the horizon.

CHAPTER ELEVEN

FRANCE

"Everything was working, that is,
except my relationship with Michel.
He hated everything German. He
hated German poetry, German music,
and especially German me!"

Lyon, France, and my first real job

The Mathieu family

AS I BOARDED THE TRAIN FROM BRAUNSCHWEIG TO LYON THAT
FEBRUARY OF 1954, MY FATHER'S SEEMINGLY SHARP GOOD-BYE
RANG IN MY EARS: "YOU ARE A HEARTLESS CREATURE!" I am sure that
he did not really believe I was a heartless creature, but I knew what he meant. My sister
had left for good, and now I was leaving him too. He would be alone with my mother
to run the family restaurant and to protect the investment he had worked so hard to
preserve through the darkest years of the war. But I was young, I had to look ahead,
and I did not see the restaurant in my future. Although I had 7 years of French in high
school, I wanted to speak it fluently; and I thought a job in France would provide the
opportunity.

As the train pulled into the station in Lyon I began to have second thoughts. Could I
do this? What if I could not? I had no experience as an au pair girl, and I knew nothing
about the family. Suddenly there they were at the train station: the whole Mathieu
family — father, mother, and my student, Michel. The parents greeted me but not
11-year-old Michel. When I offered my hand to say "hello," he turned his back. "I
don't need you," he seemed to say. And that, I was to learn, was just the beginning of
our relationship.

The family Mathieu lived in a beautiful second floor apartment at Rue de Crequi in the heart of Lyon. The floor was covered in beautiful parquet wood, and we all were encouraged to take off our shoes on entering, a ritual that was to be repeated daily. I was taken to my small but very nice room where I unpacked before returning to learn what Madame and Monsieur Mathieu would expect of me in the months ahead. Monsieur Mathieu did not say much, but Madame carefully outlined my daily chores, which included taking Michel to school, picking him up every week day, and then doing the daily shopping in the various favorite shops to which Madame would introduce me. She would provide the list and I would shop for the family.

Monsieur Mathieu, I soon learned, was a very wealthy businessman who imported and exported textiles. Madame Mathieu worked too, in a flower shop her husband had purchased for her so that she would not be bored.

The Mathieus knew that I was in Lyon to work so that I could attend the University of Lyon and study French, so on February 10 they drove me to the University, where I enrolled. I was almost 20 years old. The class I attended twice a week was made up of 12 students of eight nationalities including a Chinese fellow who always wanted to sit next to me. One day he told me that on Saturday afternoons a couple who lived near him on the bank of the Rhône River welcomed foreign students into their home to play ping-pong, billiards, and other games and to enjoy some hot chocolate and cookies. Since Saturday was my day off, I decided to try it out; and because I had fun, I went back on several occasions. Those Saturday afternoons were a special time for me, and I even improved my ping-pong game.

With Michel and his father's plane

Everything was working. I received very little pay (something like 24 marks a month), but I had a nice room and all of my food was provided as part of my compensation. Everything was working, that is, except my relationship with Michel. He hated everything German. He hated German poetry, German music, and especially German me! I was hired to teach him a language he did not want to learn and that was that. He was, however, not completely disinterested in me. He would pop into my room, unannounced, when I was dressing or undressing, and I had to tell him, "Michel, I thought all Frenchmen were gentlemen." But perhaps he was too young to understand. Eventually he did respect my privacy.

Michel did have one specific interest in the German language: he wanted to swear in German. So one day I relented and said "Okay, verdammt means damn it." But that

UNIVERSITÉ DE LYON
N° 1490

COURS AUX ÉTUDIANTS ÉTRANGERS

REÇU de Mademoiselle Fastesding de nationalité allemande
la somme de : mille francs
pour frais d'inscription aux cours pour les étrangers.

Cours intensif gradué
Cours normal 1er cycle Février
— 2me cycle
Droit d'examen

La Secrétaire générale :

Lyon, le 16.2.54

Payment for my French class at the University in Lyon

was not what he wanted to know. He wanted to know the German translation for the French word "merdre."

Immediately Michel checked his dictionary and found the translation of merdre as "Menschenkot" or "human excrement." He was overjoyed to announce his discovery to me and kept repeating over and over, "human excrement, human excrement!" I said, "Michel, if you are ever in Germany and you use that word, people will think you are an idiot and they'll laugh you out of town. But I never did tell him what he so desperately wanted to hear.

A short time later, on his 12th birthday, Michel received a gift of a new French-German dictionary. Immediately turning to the m's to find the French word and the German translation he had been looking for, he finally spotted it — "Scheisse"! I watched him go to the window. He breathed on the glass and with his finger scrawled, "Scheisse." He was so satisfied; he had solved the mystery!

Then one night as we were all sitting around the immense dining room table for dinner he dropped his fork and as he bent down to pick it up he murmured, "Scheisse!" I gasped, thinking I was surely about to be fired. Then I realized that neither of his parents spoke or understood a word of German. I was stunned when his father said, "Michel, what a beautiful word, please say it again." Michel was so proud; he loved the situation and looked at me with a devilish smile. Well, we made it through the evening, and I guess Monsieur and Madame Mathieu never did understand their son's great discovery. I kept my job and continued my studies at the University.

Although part of my job had been to walk Michel to school and pick him up after classes, he never wanted my company. He would quickly pass me by and I would walk behind him to school and back. But now that he was 12, his father said that he could go to school and come home by himself. I was relieved, as was he. He did, however, seem to enjoy playing hide and seek with me and his grandmother. Despite our rocky relationship during those months when I was his au pair girl, he cried when I said "good-bye." I kept track of Michel and am pleased to have known him as he grew into a fine young man who became a medical doctor. He married a beautiful girl and has a family of his own. Unfortunately, he became estranged from his mother and father because the young woman he chose as his wife was of the Muslim faith.

One of the highlights of my University experience and of my work for the Mathieu family was an invitation from their nephew George to attend the "Bal du Droit." George was a law student in Lyon, and this was the law students' ball. I think he had invited me in celebration of my successful completion of the French class. Now my relationship with George had come full circle from our first meeting on the Côte d'Azure to this invitation to the ball. Although it was a formal affair, I had to make do with one of the basic skirts I had brought with me. I had a wonderful time dancing although George was much shorter than I. Later in the evening a black student from the Cameroon in Africa asked me to dance, and I was shocked. Wow, this was a first! I had seen American black soldiers but was never very close to any of them. He was an excellent dancer and spoke perfect German because Cameroon had been a German protectorate before the war. I especially remember him saying that after the Germans left, everything in his country fell apart and I should be proud to be German.

> "Despite our rocky relationship during those months when I was his au pair girl, he cried when I said 'good-bye.'"

On a very important musical note, it was also during those months in Lyon that I went to a concert to hear the great jazz clarinet and soprano saxophonist Sidney Bechet. He was wonderful! I had seen a poster advertising the event to be held in a local concert hall and decided to go with one of my university girlfriends who was from Wales. Of course we bought the cheapest seats in the house, but as soon as we were seated I took my camera and went up to the front row. When I was stopped by one of the ushers I argued, "But I am a photographer from Germany" (which was certainly true). I treasure my pictures of Sidney Bechet and my memory of this fantastic concert. What a musician, what an evening! My interest in jazz was still growing.

My job in Lyon was nearly finished and I had celebrated the conclusion of my

The great Sydney Bechet and his band in Lyon

French course at the university. What next? Certainly a return to Braunschweig and the restaurant was not in the cards. As I was thinking about my options, Inge called to say she was visiting her new beau in Switzerland, that I should join her, and that I could then go on to visit our friends, those three brothers we had met on the Côte d'Azure. They were working in a chalet bar in Pralognan near Moutiers, France, and we had not seen them for a year. The same girlfriend from Wales with whom I went to see Sidney Bechet loaned me enough money for the train ticket to Lausanne where, after a long wait, I met my sister. Together we went back to Geneva and Inge gave me the money to buy a ticket to Moutiers. From there I could take a bus to Pralognan.

I said good-bye to Inge and boarded the train for what was to be a long but beautiful ride. But I had not paid attention and instead of boarding the train south to Moutiers, France, I had boarded a train north to Moutier, Switzerland. I did not discover my mistake until I got off the train in Moutier and asked the railroad agent where I could buy a bus ticket to Pralognan. "Pralognan?" He said, "There's no Pralognan here!" He took me into the station and showed me a map. My mistake was obvious. The agent was very kind and took me across the street where a woman he knew rented me a very small room in return for my last 10 francs. He then called an associate and arranged for me to return to Geneva the next morning at no cost. From there I could exchange my ticket for the right train and resume my journey.

Le Petit Chamois, the chalet where the brothers Roger, Jean, and Sylvain stayed and worked, was owned by their parents. As part of the vacation I was happy to help out wherever I could by working in the bar, ironing shirts, and darning socks. We skied when the weather was good and worked when it was not. Le Petit Chamois could well have been a setting for a romantic interlude, but there was no romance — we were just good friends. As a matter of fact, when I arrived at the chalet the oldest brother gave me a key to my room that I later gave back because, as I said, I trusted them all.

Après ski at Pralognan

"Right then and there I made the decision:
I would become an airline stewardess.
If my sister could do it, so could I."

Inge at the Brandenburg Gate

CHAPTER TWELVE

AN INVITATION THAT CHANGED MY LIFE

Arriving at Tempelhof Airport

IT HAD BEEN A WONDERFUL VACATION, BUT IT WAS TIME TO GO
HOME. The boys took me to the bus station and I boarded the same ancient machine
driven by the same grizzled driver who had brought me to Pralognan. He reminded
me of Lon Chaney in "The Hunchback of Notre Dame." The bus stopped countless
times on the way to the train station in Moutiers because in addition to his passengers,
our driver had to deliver packages and stop to have a little schnapps along the way. We
followed the serpentine road down into the valley where I caught the early morning
train to Chambery.

The railroad car was filled with men on their way to work, and I was the only person
wearing a skirt. I seemed to attract a lot of attention, so I got out a pack of cigarettes and
offered them around to the men who were sitting on the wooden benches while I sat
on one of the few real seats. In the center of the car was, of all things, a wood-burning
stove. From Chambery I went on to Geneva, Hanover, and finally Braunschweig. My
parents were happy to see me, of course; they wanted to hear about my adventures and
were pleased to have some additional help in the restaurant. Then one day, shortly after

my arrival home, the phone rang and it was for me!

It was Inge, my Pan Am stewardess sister inviting me to fly with her to Berlin. I was thrilled; it would be my very first flight, and we would stay 3 days at a hotel in Berlin. My parents were not so sure, but I begged and begged to go and as usual they finally said "okay." Little did they know they were planting the seeds of my eventual departure from the restaurant and our home in Braunschweig.

That early summer of 1954 I took the train to Hanover and the airport, where I would meet Inge and board a DC4 with about 47 other passengers for Berlin. There was no jet bridge in those days; we climbed up the stairs and into the plane. Inge went to work while I took my seat and strapped myself in. Before long we roared down the runway and lifted slowly, ever so slowly, into the air. I was so excited that I thought I would be sick, but I forgot all of that when I looked out of the window and watched us climb up through the clouds to look down on the beautiful countryside spread out below me. Flying was surely better than riding on the train, and I was not at all sick — I was thrilled! Right then and there I made the decision: I would become an airline stewardess. If my sister could do it, so could I. Anything Inge did, I wanted to do too.

> "Little did they know they were planting the seeds of my eventual departure from the restaurant and our home in Braunschweig."

I watched Inge serve drinks and snacks during what seemed a very short flight to Berlin. We landed safely at Tempelhof airport in the heart of the city. Only 6 years earlier Tempelhof had been the landing and take-off center for the Berlin Airlift that had forced the Soviets to lift their post-war blockade of the French, British, and American zones of Berlin. The Russians were trying to starve Berlin into submission, but thousands of brave young men from the Air Forces of the United States, England, Canada, Australia, New Zealand, and South Africa had risked their lives to deliver tons of food, coal, and supplies to the desperate people of West Berlin. The air lift lasted from June of 1948 through May of 1949 – more than 200,000 flights in a single year. Germany had been defeated by the Americans and the British, but in the end it was the Americans, the British, and their allies who broke the Soviet blockade and saved the people of Berlin from starvation.

Although Inge was based in Frankfurt, she had a 3-day layover in Berlin and I was her guest. She had been there before and could not wait to show me around. She wanted me to personally experience the four different occupied zones of the city (American, British, French, and Russian), which was a bona fide history lesson. We stayed in the nicest hotel I had ever seen, in the American Zone with the rest of the Pan Am crew. It was bright and cheery, there was music, and people smiled. On 2 of the 3 days we were in Berlin, Inge was scheduled to fly, but she was back in our hotel room each evening ready to go out on the town. On her day off she said, "Today we visit the East." After she explained that the rules for the trip included no makeup, no jewelry, and very plain clothes, we dressed for the occasion and boarded the "S Bahn" for East Berlin and before long were at a station called "Stalin" — Imagine that! We walked along the main street, the "Stalin Allee," which was lined with huge, new, but ugly "Soviet" style buildings that looked like a high-rise prison camp. In another way they looked like a stage set because when we looked behind the buildings, there was nothing but rubble and empty fields. I guess the Russians had put up the buildings to show off what they could do, especially during their many parades.

We continued our walk to the Siegessäule, a monument erected in 1873 to commemorate the Prussian victory in the Danish Prussian War. We watched a group of young boys in uniform, not unlike those uniforms boys wore in the Hitler Youth, marching around the monument singing Russian songs that had been translated into German. They were members of the Communist "Young Pioneers," and they were celebrating. At a side table they were being served lemonade and cookies to fill their little tummies. We could not have bought anything even if there had been something to buy because the Russians accepted only their own currency in this Soviet zone.

Inge Fasterding: Pan Am Stewardess

We had seen all we needed to see and hopped on the train back to our hotel in the American zone. What a difference! Here there were construction cranes everywhere. Many buildings had been restored or were being restored to their original condition. Shops were open and people were laughing and spending money. The city seemed to thrive with movie theaters and music, the clothes were colorful, and there was makeup! We ate in restaurants every night. I still remember one wonderful restaurant on the "Kurfürstendamm," which people simply called "Ku-Damm."

At night West Berlin was lit up and alive. One night we went to the "Badewanne," a nightclub where the performer was none other than Ella Fitzgerald. I wondered if she would recognize me from that day in Hamburg when I was so bold as to ask her for her

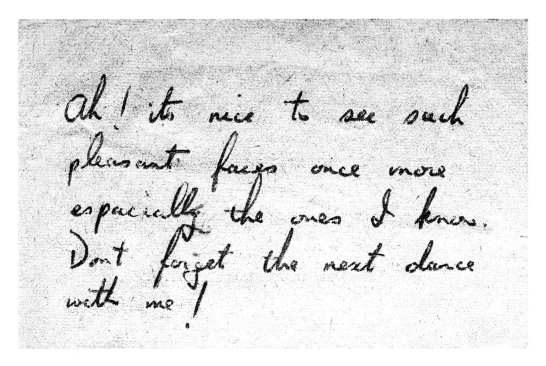

A note from one of our admirers

autograph and she was so kind to give it. I never had the chance to ask her.

Then there was "Club Resi," a bar with a huge dancefloor that we enjoyed a lot. Every table had a little street lamp with a number on it in addition to a telephone. Single men would call the number on the light and ask, "So how tall are you? Would you like to dance?" Then they would leave their number, we could call back or stand up and say, "Yes we'd like to dance, what's your name?" Inge and I loved to dance, and this was a great dance hall. There was also one other way to communicate between tables — through a hole in the wall that had a little door, next to each table. When you heard a noise, you knew that a message had arrived in a vacuum tube. You would open the door, take out the tube, and read one of your messages: "Can I dance with you?" "What's your name?" "Can I take you home?" All three of us, Inge, her stewardess friend, and I, were good dancers. We surely got our exercise that night, but we went home by ourselves. I have often thought it would be fun to have a place like "Club Resi" here in the United States. At the time I was 20 and Inge was almost 23.

Inge and I flew back to Hanover together. She went on to her job and I went out to meet my father, who had come with one of his friends to drive me back to Braunschweig. I knew he would have a thousand questions, and he did.

cutline

CHAPTER THIRTEEN

PURSUING THE DREAM

"As I looked around I thought, 'They're all much prettier and better dressed than I, and probably a lot smarter too.'"

EACH TIME I WENT OFF ON MY OWN, I SWORE I WOULD NOT RETURN TO THE RESTAURANT, BUT ONCE AGAIN, IN THAT EARLY SUMMER OF 1954, IT SEEMED TO BE THE ONLY OPTION. Not that it was unpleasant, I loved my parents; but I was eager to get on with life on my own. My work schedule at the restaurant allowed me to date lots of boys and to go out to the British and American movies, the theater, and the opera. However, my future always seemed to be on hold, and I kept thinking of Inge's life as a stewardess. I always thought positive thoughts, so I enrolled in a Spanish class because I knew that the airlines would be looking for people who could speak three foreign languages. I already had a good start in French, and Spanish seemed to be the logical next step. I thought shorthand and typing would come in handy too, so I enrolled in those classes. All of a sudden a letter came from Inge telling me that Pan Am would soon be testing stewardess candidates, I was determined I would try. The interviews were to be held in Frankfurt so I took a train and stayed overnight with my sister.

> "They're all much prettier and better dressed than I, and probably a lot smarter too."

The next morning I boarded a streetcar and then a bus to the Pan Am office. I recall that the waiting room was filled with candidates for what I knew would be very few jobs. As I looked around I thought, "They're all much prettier and better dressed than I, and probably a lot smarter too." Still I registered at the desk and when, a little later, my name was called, I was ushered through a door into a room where five or six people were waiting behind a U-shaped table. I knew they would be trying to figure out just how smart I was, when they said they had a few questions for me. The first question was, "What are the ABC states?" That was an easy one and I answered, "Argentina, Brazil, and Chile." They followed up by asking, "What's the capital of Chile?" which I knew was Santiago, although there was no way I could have prepared for their questions. One of them asked if I knew any cloud formations (I said, "Yes, cumulus") and then another asked, "Do you know any other cloud formations?" The only other formation I knew was "cirrus," and that seemed to satisfy them.

Then one of the questioners gestured and said, "Over there in the corner you'll find a tray; would you fill it with china and serve me please?" I knew they wanted to see how I walked, if I had a smile, and if I could smoothly serve from the tray. Little did they know just how many trays of food and beer I had served since I was a teenager in my father's restaurant. I certainly passed that part of the test! They asked if I had any hobbies and I said, "Yes, music, especially jazz and opera." "Name an opera and one of the characters." "La Boheme, and the character is Mimi." Finally the person in charge said, "Thank you, Miss Fasterding; nice meeting you; you'll hear back from us later." And so I left, not knowing if I had done well or not. I took the next train back to Braunschweig.

I received a polite letter from Pan Am a few weeks later saying that I had done very well during my interview and when they hired — "in the next season" — I would be on the list. Of course! I remembered that when I filled out their form I was asked my age and wrote down "20." I should have known they could not hire me until I was 21, and that would be "next season." There would be no more tests despite how well I did; but it was

> "Later I would learn that of the more than 2,000 applicants only three were chosen."

clear, I would have a year to wait – at least. Later I would learn that of the more than 2,000 applicants only three were chosen.

I was resolved to another year of helping my parents in the restaurant and dreaming about becoming a stewardess. I had made an inquiry about jobs at Lufthansa but having heard nothing back, I had decided to join a student bus tour to Paris. That seemed to be a good idea, and I had saved enough money to afford it. I persuaded my parents to let me go and they agreed, knowing there was no end to my wanderlust. One of my school friends, Maria Gropp, was interested too, and so we could go together. My good friend from Braunschweig, Uschi Wolnick, was working in Paris so I thought, "At least I will have one contact and who knows where that might lead?" Although I visited Uschi only once, the trip to Paris provided yet another opportunity. On the second day I went to the university, "Alliance Francaise," where I thought I might continue my French, and I saw an advertisement for jobs on the bulletin board. One was from a single, older woman who offered a room in exchange for someone to care for her — not a very attractive proposition, I thought. But another notice was from a Madame and Monsieur Saltzman who lived on a side street near the Arc de Triomphe. They were looking for someone to care for their 2-year-old son, Michael (whom they called Michelle), and they offered room and board and some pocket money. I decided to check it out because, after all, I was now an experienced au pair. The Salzmans were a nice couple and provided a tiny garret room in a very nice section of Paris. When the tour was over I went to work and Maria went back to Braunschweig with instructions to tell my parents I would not be coming home but had a job in Paris. Maria told me later, my mother was in tears.

One day I took young Michelle out for a walk along the Champs Elysées, and we stopped at an outdoor restaurant. I noticed a German couple nearby who were clearly interested in us and I overheard the woman say to her husband (in German), "Typical French, look at that young girl with that big baby!" She did not know that I understood her every word, and I was so tempted to say, "Yes, and I don't even know who the father is!" But I refrained, and they soon disappeared down the Champs Elysées. Knowing more than one language can be very helpful. I looked French, how could she know I was German?

I had been caring for Michelle only for a couple of weeks when on March 27, 1955, I received a telegram from Deutsche Lufthansa. The message read, "We have scheduled an interview in Hamburg to talk with you about becoming a stewardess, please confirm." What to do? I had come to love Paris and my job, but I knew that was not my future. My future was in the air, like my sister's: Whatever Inge did, I would do also…. I explained the situation to Madame Saltzman, she wished me well, and off I went to Hamburg for the interview.

"Marlis Fasterding: immediately come to Lufthansa for an interview."

Michelle on the Champs Elysées

Happy to be back to work with Flugdienst

CHAPTER FOURTEEN

BUILDING A LIFE OF MY OWN — AND A DETOUR ALONG THE WAY

"I went home to Braunschweig to tell my parents that I was ready to fly again, and they were shocked."

Two flying sisters, 1956

I THOUGHT THE OFFER HAD TO BE SERIOUS BECAUSE, ALONG WITH THE INVITATION TO COME FOR AN INTERVIEW, I HAD RECEIVED AN AIRLINE TICKET. I flew from Paris directly to the Hamburg Fuhlsbüttel airport. The next day I entered another room full of people to take another test. This time I had to read humorous stories from three different Reader's Digest magazines, one in English, one in French, and one in Spanish. I got through all of them even though my Spanish was still a little weak. The most difficult part was to explain "why" the joke was funny in each of the three languages. I do not remember what the stories were about, but I do recall that I promised I would take lessons to improve my Spanish. Once again they measured my height and watched me walk, and at the end of the test they said, "We'll let you know our decision in a few days."

As it turned out Inge was now in a position to find out what was going on. Although she had been enjoying her work with Pan Am, her flights had been limited to German cities and Vienna and served business people and refugees. She had been waiting to be sure that Lufthansa had become a solid organization offering international service before she applied to be part of their second class of stewardesses. When she was sure, she made the move and was hired without a test. As a Lufthansa stewardess she was in a position to find out just what was going on with my test and application.

Inge quickly found out that the person in charge of my application was the Lufthansa Chief Stewardess, Ursula Tautz (for some reason called "Peter Tautz"). This woman was so envious of Inge's current beau that she had secretly seen to it that I did not get the job. When Inge heard from one of the stewards that I did not make the

A chance meeting and a newspaper photo: Robert, Inge, and I in Frankfurt

final list, she was very upset. She did not know the reason but was determined to do something about it. When she was at the airport the next day, one of the people who had interviewed me congratulated Inge and said, "Now we have two from your family!" Inge was confused. She went to the Chief Stewardess, Ms. Tautz, who said she had heard only that I had done very well and did not understand why I was not in the next class. Clearly she had made the decision and was engaged in a cover-up. In time, Inge figured it out but could do nothing about it. However, I was not going to let this little romantic intrigue interrupt my career.

The next day I got the news. I was being offered a job, not with Lufthansa but with Deutsche Lufttransport, a subsidiary of Lufthansa that flew regional and charter flights. I accepted the job immediately even though Inge kept saying that she would continue to straighten things out with Lufthansa, that she knew Ursula Tautz because they flew together at Pan Am. Even so, she was unsuccessful and I began training with Deutsche Lufttransport.

Because we both were stationed in Hamburg, Inge and I were able to share a room. It was a terrible place in the basement of an old building, but because Hamburg was a mess after the war, I guess we were lucky to find it. However, when we noticed a new building going up and there was an opportunity to put a deposit on a new apartment, we asked my father for help and he gave us the money we needed. We moved in shortly thereafter and lived there together for nearly a year. It was so much better than the old place. My training stewardess was a young woman around my age named Ursula or "Usch" Schröder. In time, we would become good friends and later would share apartments in Frankfurt. But I am getting ahead of my story.

My first flight was to Copenhagen on a DC3. It was an evening flight and I still remember looking down to see all of the beautiful lights as we approached the city. Our captain, Schönberger, had never flown into Copenhagen before. I guess that was the reason for his rather "strange" landing. We descended to land but as we approached the runway Captain Schönberger pulled up and flew in a big circle before descending

a second time. Then once again he pulled up and once again he went around. I thought nothing of it, only perhaps that he was checking his tires. On the third try we touched down and I looked over at Usch and saw that she was pale as a bedsheet and not too happy. For her it had been a white knuckle flight and she was noticeably scared. Me? I was okay; I did not know any better because it was my first flight with Deutsche Lufttransport. Captain Schönberger, the

Co-Pilot, the Navigator, Usch, and I all stayed overnight in a hotel in the city and the next day went together to wonderful festive Tivoli Gardens. I remembered the place well from my days in Copenhagen years earlier when I was an exchange student.

My next flight and many more to come would be to Palma de Mallorca. One of them was unlike any of the others. It was a rainy day in Hamburg, and part of my job was to escort the passengers from the terminal to the plane. Although I had an umbrella, I was soaked. After everyone was seated we strapped ourselves in and the plane lifted off. On the DC3 the stewardess seat was right next to the main passenger door that never closed properly and an ice cold draft blew against my seat all the way to Palma. It was very cold and I was very wet — not a good combination. Still, I performed my service and the passengers were happy. We landed in Palma and went directly to the Jaime Primero Hotel for the night. It was the first hotel built in Palma and, as I remember, somewhat "basic."

During the night I developed a temperature and began to shake. The cold would just not go away and I realized I was very sick. I called the Captain and told him there was no way I could fly back with him; I just could not get out of bed. "Oh no," he said, "You're not staying here in this place; you're coming home with us!" And so I forced myself to get dressed and go to the airport.

The flight home was terrible. I tried to focus on my job but when all of the passengers had left and our caterer came on board I said, "Please get me a taxi, I have to get home; I'm really sick." I could not even do the accounting of the items I had sold on the flight. After the caterer found me a taxi, I told the driver where I lived and gave him the key to my apartment. He dropped me off at the front door and somehow I made it upstairs and into bed. A day later, Inge arrived home from Brazil to find me in bed fully dressed in my uniform. I had not moved in 24 hours.

"A day later, Inge arrived home from Brazil to find me in bed fully dressed in my uniform. I had not moved in 24 hours."

Inge really did not know what to do with me except to seek help from a physician she knew who treated people with herbs. We linked arms and walked down the street to his office. He gave us some herbal powder that I took back to the apartment. I took it but it had no effect. I was terribly weak and could only go back to bed.

Inge had to go back to work so she called our mother in Braunschweig, who came by train to Hamburg to take care of me. I still remember the hot potatoes she wrapped in a towel and put on my chest. It certainly seemed like a strange treatment, but it worked. Gradually my breathing improved, although I was soon to learn from the doctor, in addition to pneumonia and pleurisy, was that I had contracted a condition called "ulcerative colitis," which was to be with me well into the future. We learned of my condition from Dr. Weiss, Chief Physician at the Elin Hospital. He came to the apartment and advised that I go to the hospital immediately. After hearing my weak but firm response ("No, I do not want to go to the hospital!"), Dr. Weiss looked me straight in the eye and said, "Then you will die!" Within minutes the doctor and his assistant had rolled me onto a stretcher and had carried me out to a car. Accompanied by my mother and against my wishes, I was on my way to the hospital, where the doctors and nurses tried everything. I had four person-to-person blood transfusions, one from a woman who said she ate raw liver and another from a butcher who drank cow's blood. I think I became even sicker when they told me why their blood was so rich. The nurses gave me so many injections of iron that they eventually had a difficult time finding veins and ended up using my feet.

"You are too young to die."

I was in a single room, and after 2 months I was pounding on the wall. I just did not want to live any more. Then one night one of the nurses, Lydia Koch, heard me and came into the room. She had worked all day and was ready to go home. Although she was dead tired, she stayed and prayed with me the entire night. I remember her saying, "You are too young to die." Lydia was like an angel sitting next to me. In time I grew very quiet, and I guess I decided she was right. The next day or so my father arrived from Braunschweig, took one look at me, and began to cry. I had seen my father cry only twice before, when Braunschweig was in flames and when my little brother died. They said that when I was in the hospital I looked like Gandhi, although I had long blond braids because I had not cut my hair since I became sick that night on the airplane.

I knew I was getting better when they took me out to the back garden in a wheelchair. It was fall and the leaves were just beginning to come down; I had been in the hospital for nearly 4 months! I still have the papers for my release. They pronounced me well enough to go home

Lydia Koch

but could not make any promises about the colitis. They said it could return as a result of excitement, of being very happy or very sad and that I should not eat fresh produce such as strawberries or lettuce.

My parents had made arrangements for me to go from the hospital to a well-known "Kurort," not a full spa but a place where people went on holiday. The Kurort was in Ruhpolding, Bavaria, a ski resort. They had bought me a ticket on a vacation train from Hanover, and when I arrived there was a brass band at the station to welcome us – not only for me, of course, but for all of the vacationers. I had a nice room that I shared with a girl I had never seen before, and little by little, thanks to the good air in the mountains, my strength returned and I was soon ready to leave. I telephoned Usch Schröder in Frankfurt, and she invited me to stay with her on my way home. Usch had changed from Deutsche Lufttransport to Flugdienst, which was soon to become Condor Airlines. She was very excited about the new company, a subsidiary of Lufthansa; and she persuaded me that my best tonic would be to go back to work, for Flugdienst. When I agreed she arranged an interview, and I was hired on the spot.

I went home to Braunschweig to tell my parents that I was ready to fly again, and they were shocked. They could not believe that I would go back to flying after all I had been through, but I had a strong will and knew what I wanted. As I said, eventually

Ruhpolding: high in the Bavarian Alps

Flugdienst would become Condor, the leisure airline of Thomas Cook AG. Its other partners were Norddeutcher Lloyd, Hamburg-America Line, Lufthansa, and Deutsche Bundesbahn. Based on that merger, my new employer was owned by a travel company, a shipping company, a steamship company, an airline, and a train company. Delighted to be with Condor, Usch and I were poised to have the time of our lives!

During this time Inge was already having the time of her life travelling the world for Lufthansa. She flew to the capitals of Europe and the Middle East, Africa, South America, and the United States. On April 21, 1956, Inge was privileged to make the opening flight to Chicago on a Lufthansa Super Constellation. At the time it was the largest, fastest passenger plane in the

My wonderful rest in Ruhpolding

world. Still, the flight took 22 hours and required refueling stops in Shannon, Goose Bay/Gander, and Montreal.

Inge spent a full week in Chicago and with the rest of her crew was treated like a celebrity. They attended receptions and parties, paid visits to the local German clubs, and went to a baseball game at Wrigley Field at the invitation of the Wrigley family. Inge's job with Lufthansa had lots of wonderful benefits, not the least of which was flying with the handsome head purser of the airline, Robert Huhn. They had enjoyed working a number of flights together when, during a stopover in Rio de Janeiro, Robert asked Inge to marry him. She told me the news as soon as she could and asked me to be a witness. I was thrilled for her!

"Inge spent a full week in Chicago and with the rest of her crew was treated like a celebrity."

They continued to fly, sometimes together, and Robert was selected to be the steward for German Chancellor Konrad Adenauer's state visits abroad. They were married in 1957 with a civil service in Hamburg on August 23 and a church service on September 22 in Robert's family hometown of Oberwinter above the Rhine River, very near Bonn. Their fabulous reception was at the Petersberg

Usch Schröeder and I flew the opening flights of our new Convair aircraft above Frankfurt, Cologne, Hanover, Hamburg, Stuttgart, Nuremberg, and Düssledorf in 1958.

Opening flight to Gibraltar with British crew members

Inge and Robert

Petersberg Hotel dramatically perched high on a mountain top with a clear view of the Rhine, the city of Bonn, and, in good weather, the steeples of the dome in Cologne. For their honeymoon they climbed aboard an Air France Super Connie and flew all the way around the world. It must have been a honeymoon to end all honeymoons! On their arrival home Inge retired and Robert moved to a Lufthansa administrative job in Bonn, where he continued to oversee Lufthansa service for Chancellor Konrad Adenauer's state visits. They settled in Oberwinter and Robert continued his hobby as a competitive race car driver, which he had begun with "Scuderia Lufthansa," the Lufthansa racing team, earlier in his career. Inge and Robert raised three children, Silke, Heike, and Jens, all of whom followed their parents' lead working for Lufthansa. Silke and Heike circled the world many times over as career stewardesses.

Opening flight to Chicago: Inge (left) and Gisela Krag arrive at Midway airport

Famous driver Juan Manuel Fangio (right) congratulates Robert on his victory in the 1000-km race at the Nürburgring

The amazing "Connie"

The Viking

CHAPTER FIFTEEN

AIRBORNE — ONCE AGAIN

"I had come to know company CEO Eberhard von Brauchitsch quite well but was still surprised when he called me into his office to say, 'Marlis Fasterding, I need you to become our Chief Stewardess....'"

MY CAREER WITH FLUGDIENST BEGAN OFFICIALLY ON APRIL 13, 1957, BUT THE ONLY RECORD I CAN FIND INDICATES THAT MY FIRST FLIGHT WAS ON MAY 10. Once again our pilot was Captain Schönberger, who had moved from Lufttransport to Flugdienst, as had I. We carried some 30 passengers aboard a "Viking," the aircraft that had been converted to passenger service from the old British "Wellington" bomber used during the war. How ironic, that I first knew it from above and now I am in it! That first flight left Düsseldorf for Palma Mallorca with stops in Hamburg, Frankfurt, and Lyon. The airplanes were quite slow in those days. I can still remember my surprise when we rolled to a stop at the Palma airport and I opened the door to see a crowd of people who had come to welcome us. Passenger flights were still a novelty in those days, and for something to do people often came out to the airport just to watch the planes land. So our landing that day was not an unusual event at all.

Over the next 2 years I would fly with Condor and Lufthansa, Condor being a subsidiary of Lufthansa. Regardless of whether the flight was Condor or Lufthansa, we stewardesses all wore the same uniforms. Over those years I carefully recorded each and every flight in my "Flugbuch" or flight log book, which I still have. What a time that

(L to R) Captain Mueller, Captain von der Burg, Navigator Jessberger

was! Even today the destinations read like a romantic tour of Europe and the Middle East. Of course we flew to all of the major German cities — Frankfurt, Düsseldorf, Munich, Stuttgart, Nuremberg, Cologne, Hanover, and Hamburg – as well as all the major cities of Europe. But there were also other more exotic destinations such as Mallorca, Gibraltar, Casablanca, Tangier, Tenerife, Barcelona, Lyon, and Marseilles. Additional stops included Athens, Istanbul, Brindisi on the heel of Italy, Cairo, and eventually the United States. But once again, I am getting ahead of my story.

In the beginning Condor had only five stewardesses, but more were added when the airline purchased four 40-passenger Convair aircraft from the Dutch airline KLM. With the exception of special charter flights, only one stewardess was assigned to each airplane. Many of the flights were memorable. For example, on September 21, 1957, the German sail training ship "Pamir" was caught in a fierce hurricane and sank off the Azores. Of the 86 crew and cadets aboard, only five survived. On September 29, one of the Condor "Vikings" was dispatched to pick up the five survivors in Casablanca and take them home to Hamburg. I was the stewardess and I will never forget that 8-hour trip. The young cadets were in terrible shape, and we had members of the press aboard who were constantly pressuring them for details of the sinking. I finally brought the survivors, one at a time, to the cockpit where they could have something to eat away from those insensitive press people.

On October 15, 1957, we flew the German National track and field team to Budapest where they were to compete against the Hungarians. It was the first such international event to be held after the war. I remember the trip because when we landed and I opened the cabin door, I was met by six armed soldiers. "We want to speak with your captain!" they demanded. When I told Captain Rudolphi he said, "Oh yes, I was here once before, during the war. I suppose they want to talk with me about that." So off he went with the soldiers. We all were very concerned, but 20 minutes later he returned with a smile on his face. We were greatly relieved and proceeded to disembark.

In Budapest the members of the press, the team physicians, and the crew stayed in a wonderful hotel on Margarit Island in the middle of the city. This hotel had the most marvelous indoor swimming pool that produced its own waves. I had never seen anything like it and had a great time swimming in the waves. We were invited to attend the track meet and I went with Captain Rudolphi, Co-Pilot von der Burg, and our navigator, Wöst.

That stayover in Budapest also included a tour of a local winery after the team had gone off to practice. This was another new experience for me, so I carefully watched the manager as he went from barrel to barrel tasting with us the different vintages of Tokai, the famous wine of Hungary. I noticed that with each

At the track meet with (L to R) Wöst, Rudolphi, and von der Burg

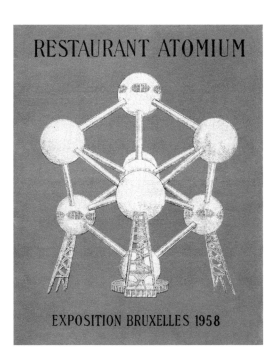

A wonderful evening at the Atomium

The German track team in Budapest

tasting he spit the wine out onto the sandy floor. I, but not the press or the physicians, did the same. Later, when we came up out of the cellar, the fresh air made most of them empty their stomachs onto the ground. I asked them, "What's the matter, can't you drink a little wine?" I was the smart one.

In 1958 there were a number of flights to the wonderful Brussels World's Fair, where we were free to enjoy the sights. On one occasion we had dinner at a restaurant located high in the "Atomium," the bright aluminum futuristic structure that was the theme building of the fair. We enjoyed quite a wonderful dinner! We drank Chateau Magdelene, St. Emilion 1953, ate a main course of sole meunier; and ended with soufflé glacé au Grand Marnier for dessert. I still have the menu, which includes the signatures of all of my dinner companions and friends (who were the first to call me "Lis").

As we approached Palma Mallorca on one of our many flights there, I looked down to see a huge American aircraft carrier along with two heavy cruisers and many other ships in the harbor. It was a magnificent sight! I decided we had to go aboard that carrier, which I learned from our pilot was the "Essex." Our pilot also said, "Impossible!" But as usual, I was determined and so I bet him a bottle of cognac that I would arrange a tour of the "Essex" for our entire crew. It was morning and after we landed we all went

Exploring the Brussels World's Fair

off to check in at the hotel where we would stay that night. I told the crew to get ready and off I went to the harbor, which was nearby.

I watched as rubber boats brought the enlisted men ashore, and I approached one of them: "Any chance that you could take me and my crew aboard?" I asked, looking very professional in my uniform. The sailors said they could not possibly give us permission to come aboard and I should wait for one of the officers. One arrived in the next tender, and with my very best smile I asked if we might tour the ship. "Oh no," he said, "we only take the people who live here in Palma out to see the ship, and we don't take them aboard, we just circle around with one of our tenders to give them a look. And besides, it's not Sunday, we only take guests out to the ship on Sundays." I gave him my "Please sir" smile and he said, "Well, maybe I can arrange something if you will bring your crew here to the harbor this afternoon; I'll see what I can do. I'll have a tender then and we can go around the ship."

I had opened the door, and so I went back to the hotel to collect my crew. I told them they would be able to "see" the Essex; I had no intention of giving up on a personal tour of the ship. The young lieutenant welcomed us aboard his tender and we headed out to the huge aircraft carrier in the harbor. I asked him if he would "please" try to get us aboard because I did not want to lose a bet I had made with our captain. I

USS Essex

revealed that I had bet the captain I would arrange for us all to go aboard the ship, and the prize was a bottle of cognac. I sensed that I was winning when we came closer to the huge ship and the lieutenant waved to another officer at the railing that he wanted to bring us aboard. Success!

The only way to get aboard the ship was to climb a rope ladder and it was a long, long way up. I had never climbed a rope ladder and I was in a skirt, so I asked if I could go last, which I did with the exception of one of the sailors who said he had to go last for "safety" reasons. I believed him, and of course I wanted to be safe.

The ship was huge! As we began the personal tour that I had promised our crew, we learned that 2,000 sailors were on board, not counting those who flew and cared for the airplanes. The USS Essex was some 820 feet long and was very fast. It could cruise at 32 knots — not as fast as our airplanes, but for a ship that size, very fast! Onboard were a basketball court (maybe two), a bakery, a print shop, and a huge cafeteria or "galley" where the crew had to eat in three shifts because there were so many of them. We were personally escorted throughout the ship just as I had promised. I tried to cover up my "very satisfied" smile, but the captain knew he had lost our bet. The next day before flying back to Frankfurt, he presented me with my winning bottle of cognac.

Passenger flights in those days were still a new experience for most people, and all

Technische Daten der Convair:

Hersteller: Consolidated Vultee Aircraft Corporation U. S. A.
Motoren: Pratt and Whitney R-2800 CA 18
Motorenleistung: 2400 PS pro Motor
Benzinverbrauch: etwa 600 l pro Flugstunde im Durchschnitt
Fassungsvermögen der Benzintanks: 3785 l
Länge: 22,75 m   Höhe: 8,20 m
Tragflächenspannweite: ca. 28 m
Druckkabinen und Frischluftregelung von: Airesearch U. S. A.
Maximales Startgewicht: 19 300 kg
Reisegeschwindigkeit: ca. 400 km/h
Kabinenkapazität: 40 Sitze
Zusätzliche Frachtkapazität: 1660 kg (Frachtvolumen: 9,5 Kubikmeter)

Deutsche Flugdienst GmbH., Frankfurt am Main - Flughafen · Bürogebäude Ost · Fernruf 698213 / 698229 · Fernschreiber 041-2038

Brochure describing the Convair

A special visit to the Volkswagen plant in Wolfsburg

of our passengers seemed very happy to be flying with us. I remember that we received our first rave reviews from a group of automobile businessmen on a charter flight to Wolfsburg. They complimented Condor on every aspect of the trip, "…especially the two stewardesses that took such good care of us aboard the plane. It was a fantastic trip and we thank you!" As an added plus we were invited to go along with them to tour the Volkswagen factory, and that was really fascinating. Being a stewardess for Condor and Lufthansa opened a great many doors and provided a host of new experiences.

On November 1, 1957, I had been with Condor for 7 months. I had come to know company CEO Eberhard von Brauchitsch quite well but was still surprised when he called me into his office to say, "Marlis Fasterding, I need you to become our Chief Stewardess, to recruit and train new stewardesses for the company." And so it happened: out of the air and into the office. At that time you may recall that we had only five stewardesses and needed to expand because Condor had bought four new Convairs from KLM. When the company had placed an advertisement in the newspapers, the applications arrived in stacks. My job was to evaluate them and to write letters informing the successful candidates that they were to be called for interviews.

I accepted this "promotion" reluctantly and after only 1 month told Mr. von Brauchitsch that I really wanted to get back into the air. He said, "Okay, you can be Chief Stewardess and continue to fly. Our airline is also training new pilots and

One of our first Convairs

you can fly with the new candidates to Stuttgart and see how they do in the air before you make your final selection. How many [applicants] do you have?" "Twelve," I replied. A few became air sick on the flight to Stuttgart and had to be eliminated, but over the next 2 months I met my quota of candidates whom I thought were very good.

Once they had been selected, I continued to supervise the new stewardesses as they trained aboard the planes on actual trips. They learned how to behave in the air, about flight protocol, emergency procedures, and how to do their own catering in foreign locations. I briefed them on how to wear their uniform, gave them the name of a salon where they could learn about makeup, and told them always to avoid jewelry as well as conversation about politics and religion. These were the company rules. The stewardesses were in charge of the passengers and whenever there was a delay, which was often, it was our job to entertain them.

On December 20, 1957, we took off from Frankfurt on a 16-day Condor tour that would include stops in Brindisi, Athens, Istanbul, Beirut, Jerusalem, Cairo, Benina in Tripoli, Tunis, Tangier, Lisbon, and Madrid before returning to Germany. Quite a trip and quite an adventure! We were scheduled to be in Jerusalem on Christmas day!

The fourth leg of the trip, from Istanbul to Beirut was very short. We landed on December 24 during the day and went

A stop in Istanbul

off to our hotel where we would spend the night. The "Riviera" hotel was beautiful; right on the beach looking out on the deep blue waters of the Mediterranean. Beirut was a place where you could go swimming in the morning and drive up to Baalbek to go skiing in the afternoon. I was impressed!

In Germany we celebrate Christmas on Christmas Eve by being together, lighting real candles on the Christmas tree, and exchanging gifts. So I had brought along a sprig from a Christmas tree, a candle, two little angels, and gifts for the crew. I put all of these items on a table and drew the curtains in my room. I called the crew together and gave out the presents I had brought for the four men – Captain Rudolphi, Co-Pilot Geissler, Wollweber the mechanic, and Reynders the navigator. As we all were singing "O Tannenbaum," I noticed that our mechanic was crying and so I asked, "What's wrong?" Well, he had six children at home in Germany and he wanted to be with them for Christmas, even though he knew he could not be. Captain Rudolphi broke the mood: "Let's go to the beach and have some fun, we can all have Christmas when we get back to Germany."

Then the phone rang. It was our Station Manager, a Lebanese fellow named Mr. Katuri who was calling to invite me to go into the heart of the city to the King George Hotel, which he said had the best disco in all of Lebanon. He would pick me up at 7:00 PM. Naturally I called Captain Rudolphi to ask what he thought, and he said, "It should be great fun." "Yes," I said, "but I don't want to go alone, why don't you come along?"

So at 7:00 I came down in the elevator with my Captain. Mr. Katuri was in the lobby and was obviously not happy to see that we would be a party of three. He led us out to a big black car waiting in front of the hotel and opened the front door for Captain Ruldolphi. I was ushered into the back seat with our host. It did not take long for Mr. Katuri to put his arm around my shoulder and then his hand on my knee while, over and over again, I resisted his "overtures." Before long we arrived at the hotel and went downstairs to

Our arrival in Jerusalem

the disco called "Cave du Roi," where a live band was playing popular music. Katuri asked me to dance but I declined saying that I did not know how, Captain Rudolphi smiled; he could not believe what was going on. When I had a chance I explained a little further and told him I would not sit in the back seat on the way home. He clearly understood and when it was time to get back in the car, he climbed into the back seat with Katuri and I sat up front with the driver.

Katuri was so angry that he hardly spoke to me. It seemed that he would never give up, however. I was in my room only a short time when the phone rang and it was he. I was polite and said we were flying out tomorrow and I was very tired. I hung up and when the phone rang again. I did not answer.

The next morning we were preparing the plane for takeoff and I was in my galley. All of the caterers had left and who came up the ladder into the plane but a very angry Mr. Katuri. "You are a stupid girl!" he exclaimed. "I could have given you a gold bracelet or anything else made of gold; you are so stupid!" I knew I was not "stupid," but smart. I was very proud of having handled a difficult situation as I did. I will never forget Mr. Katuri; perhaps he also remembers me.

December 25, 1957, was to be my very first Christmas away from home. And it would most certainly be a Christmas to remember. We landed in Jerusalem and learned that our trip would be unexpectedly delayed. It was not a

Cairo 1957

problem, except that no hotel arrangements had been made for us or our passengers… and it was Christmas. Because it was the crew's and our tour guides' responsibility to care for the passengers, we all began making telephone calls to find a hotel. Meanwhile, our tour guide arranged for a bus to take the passengers sightseeing around Jerusalem. They of course had no idea what was going on. Although every hotel was booked, we finally found one — "Casa Nova"— that agreed to accommodate all of us, passengers and crew. "Ah, Casa Nova, the New House," said our captain. "Sounds good!" What I did not tell him, however, was that Casa Nova was not really a hotel, it was a monastery! We were to be guests of the monks who lived there and had graciously agreed to come to our aid. I guess they thought it was their Christian duty.

We arrived and were directed to our rooms, which were like little cells, very basic with only a bed and a sink. Given the circumstances, we were happy to be here. When it was time for dinner we all assembled around a long rough table as the monks served us a kind of stew or porridge. They came around with a large bowl and spooned whatever it was onto our plates. We were thankful to be fed. After the food, along came the wine maker monk of the monastery with a large pitcher full of wine; I still remember his very red nose and thinking to myself that he clearly enjoyed his work. We settled into the comfort of Casa Nova for the evening with lights out at 10:00 and no heat! Night in the desert was bitterly cold, and I unpacked all of my clothes and dressed for bed to keep warm.

> "'Ah, Casa Nova, the New House,' said our captain. 'Sounds good!' What I did not tell him, however, was that Casa Nova was not really a hotel, it was a monastery!"

The next day the crew and I set out on our own. We hired a driver and a small minibus to take us from Jerusalem to Bethlehem. After all, it was the day after Christmas. Our driver took us to a place where the local monks said Jesus was born. We got out of our little bus and immediately encountered a monk who asked us for money. We gave him a few coins and he escorted us inside, which was very peaceful. The monk followed us inside and described the altars: one Christian, one Orthodox, and possibly a third. We exited into a small shop where I bought an olive wood necklace studded with silver – or at least they said it was silver. The monk returned to direct us across the street to a place he called the "Milk Grotto." He said that was where Joseph and Mary were hiding with the baby. Although no one wanted to go with me, I of course went.

Inside was a stone about 2 or 3 feet high and on top of it was a statue of Mary and baby Jesus. Next to the stone was a stand with little packets containing a white powder.

My stubborn camel

The monk said that I should buy one of the packets because it would help me to get pregnant. I did not buy any. As we left the grottos we were besieged by a number of young boys with their hands outstretched calling for "bakchis!" One little boy had such a miserable and sad expression on his face that I wanted to give him some money. Because I had no coins left, I borrowed some from one of our crew and gave them to the boy. As we left I looked back over my shoulder and there he was jumping up and down for joy. I had fallen for his pitch! After a few hours our minibus took us back to the Casa Nova to collect our things for the next leg of our journey.

From Jerusalem it was a short hop to Cairo, where we would stay over before going on to Tunis. Cairo had no modern hotels like Sheraton or Hilton, so we checked into the best Egyptian hotel we could find called the "Abdin Palace Hotel." The men in our crew wanted to see Egyptian belly dancers, and when I overheard them making an inquiry at the desk, I told them I wanted to go too. "But the belly dancers are only for men," said one of them. I did not care; if they were going, I was going too; and so I persuaded them to take me along. We took a taxi to a place called "Scheherazade," a large upstairs room where we joined an eager audience of Egyptian men. In the back of the room we sat on decorated leather hassocks and to my greatest amazement saw that the heavier the belly dancer, the greater the applause. The belly dancing I had seen in films featured girls who were skinny. Not these! Here it was the bigger the better!

"The belly dancing I had seen in films featured girls who were skinny. Not these! Here it was the bigger the better!"

The next day we departed Cairo for Tripoli and Tunis. When the passengers were asleep, dead tired from all their sightseeing, Captain Rudolphi called me into the cockpit and asked, "How would you like to fly the plane?" I was thrilled! I loved flying, and the idea of taking the controls was all the more exciting. I flew the Convair for 3 full minutes and was very proud of myself. Then Captain Ruldophi took over and we landed in Tripoli. We stayed overnight and as we were preparing to leave the next morning, the captain burst my bubble by telling me, "Fasterding, you flew the plane very well yesterday because, to tell you the truth, all the while you were at the controls the plane was on autopilot." I could have strangled him! Still, that 16-day trip around the Mediterranean had to be one of my most memorable ever.

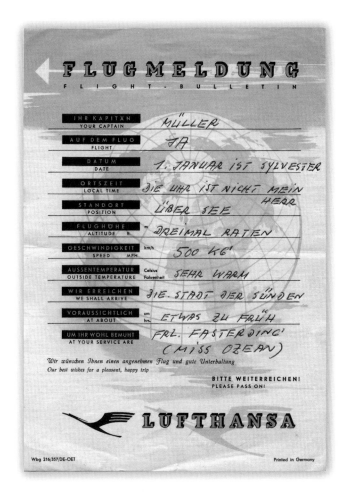

We had no microphone in the cabin so the Captains filled out the "Flugmeldung" or "Flight Bulletin" for every trip. The Captain passed the bulletin out of the cockpit to the stewardess and the stewardess handed it to the passenger in the first row who passed it to the next row and so on. This took the place of the announcements now routine on all airlines.

Our bulletins, however, often reflected the "playful" and "irreverent" personality of the Captains. This one by Captain Müller includes the following information:

Flight: Yes

Local Time: The clock is not my master

Position: Above the sea

Altitude: You may guess three times

Speed: 500 kg

Outside Temperature: Very warm

We shall arrive: In the "sin" city

At about: A little too early

At your service: Miss Fasterding (Miss Ocean)

Training flight with Trudi Weiss (top left), Captains Schorries and Mac Dougall (center), and I looking on

CHAPTER SIXTEEN

OUR FLYING FAMILY

"We were proud of our airline and proud to wear our uniforms. But above all, we were proud to be a family."

A Lufthansa/Condor family portrait: March 1, 1958
(Top – von der Burg, Schorries; Middle – Elke Cramer, myself; Bottom – Jessberger)

YES, FLYING WAS A JOB AND EVEN A CAREER, BUT IT WAS SO MUCH MORE. Looking back, those of us who flew together in those primitive machines during those early post-war days of German passenger flights soon became a family. We all were in it together; there was a unique sense of excitement and comradery because everything was new. We were pioneers helping to bring our country back from the brink and making the world just a little more civilized. We were proud of our airline and proud to wear our uniforms. But above all, we were proud to be a family. The flight crews would grow to 25 and 30 in just a couple of years.

The work was hard and we never knew what to expect. On all of the flights to Tétouan in Morocco we had to off-load all of the dishes and glasses from the plane and take them with us to the hotel where they were cleaned. The next morning we had to collect everything and transport it back to the plane. Sometimes we had to order food during a stop so we would have something to serve our passengers. I even helped load ballast into the plane, and went once to the tower to check the weather.

On our flights from Germany to Tenerife in the Canary Islands, we always stayed overnight at the crew hotel in Tétouan. I always collected any items of food like fruit and cookies, crackers, and sugar cubes that the passengers had not used and put them in sick bags to take to the hotel for the employees. I did this often, and after the first time, I was met with big smiles on every arrival. On one occasion the head waiter at the hotel said, "When you return tomorrow from Tenerife, I would like to invite you to my house." We had a delay on the way back the next night, and the runway had to be illuminated by fires in large oil drums, but the landing was smooth. We were dead tired when we arrived late at the hotel, and there was the head waiter to welcome us back. The crew did not want to go to his house, but I insisted we honor his invitation.

It was his night off from the hotel. We walked through a very narrow street, past white-washed houses, until he opened the small front door to his home. We did not know what to expect and were surprised to be welcomed by a beautiful garden. Inside, on the front step, he was heating a large kettle of boiling water to which he added stalks of fresh mint. We went up one step to a large room and sat on soft sofas covered with oriental carpets. He told us about his family and about how his father had married four wives, two of whom had died. We asked to meet his mother, and he went to bring her into the room. Her face was completely veiled, but she undid her veil to smile and greet each of us before buttoning up again and bidding us good night. Our waiter friend told us about the traditional Moroccan arranged wedding in which young girls are chosen to be the wives of old men without ever seeing their future husbands. We were amazed. The evening was another of those unique cultural experiences I never would have had except for my work as a stewardess.

> "'A waiter asked if I was for sale or trade. 'Maybe,' said the Captain, 'what do you offer?'"

We got to know a number of people at the hotel. A waiter once asked the Captain if I was "for sale or trade." "Maybe," said the Captain. "What do you offer?" The waiter began by offering a goat, but the Captain said, "No, that's not enough." So he added a second and a third goat, but the Captain said, "No, no, you've got to do better than that, at least a camel." The waiter came close to the Captain and whispered into his ear, "Two?" "No, no, at least three," said the Captain in a loud voice. Well, the highest the waiter would go was one camel, and that ended the bidding. I was safe, and we all had a good laugh. It was all very Moroccan and very funny.

Condor flew many charter flights, including three from Düsseldorf to Oslo in the summer of 1958 when the world semi-finals in soccer ("Fussball") were being held. I was the stewardess on one of these flights, and our passengers were a group of very

Felix Müller was a great pilot and a good friend.

high-class businessmen from the Rhine/Ruhr manufacturing district. After the game we flew them on to Stockholm to watch the championship match between Sweden and Brazil.

I knew the game would be important because the great Brazilian player "Pele" would be on the field. He was already a hero in Brazil and a celebrity in world soccer, and I was determined to see him play. Of course all of our passengers had tickets, but not our crew. However, true to form, I would see what I could do about that.

I went to the Captain and said, "We all must wear our uniforms to the stadium and I will get us in." "Ha!" he replied. "This match has been sold out for months, where do you think you're going to get tickets?" Well, he did join the rest of the crew and came with me to the stadium, everyone still wearing their uniforms. While they waited outside I set off on a tour around the stadium and finally found a friendly face with a white beard. He looked a little like Santa Claus. I told him my "story," that I was the chief stewardess and my crew was outside on the bench waiting to check with our passengers for tickets. "So, where are the passengers?" he said. "I don't know, they are inside somewhere and they have our tickets." Just another little white lie I thought could do no harm. "I'm sorry" he said, "but if you don't even know what section they're in, I don't know what I can do to help." I smiled and asked, "Maybe we could sit on the stone steps?" He disappeared inside the stadium and in a short time returned to wave us in. No one believed it but they should have known that my motto was the same as Winston Churchill's: "Never give up!" My crew was amazed and delighted with our good luck. We arranged ourselves one behind the other on the stone steps of the stadium when, to our great surprise, the nice people on the wooden benches moved over to make room for us in real seats. We then watched the most spectacular soccer game ever. Pele was playing for Brazil and we were in the stands. He of course played his usual great game, but in the end Sweden won the world championship. The stomping and cheering of the home team crowd was deafening.

When World War II ended, Finland and Germany agreed on a friendly exchange of badly wounded soldiers. Condor was selected to fly the Finish veterans from Frankfurt back to Helsinki where a group of German veterans then came aboard for the return trip to Frankfurt. It was a diplomatic exchange between two countries that had been at war just a few years earlier. The veterans were in a splendid mood, happy to have survived the war and telling lots of army jokes. I must have blushed. I remember asking some of the badly wounded soldiers whether I could help cut their food but despite the obvious difficulty, each one refused saying, "I can do it myself."

> "As we flew over the Finland Lake District we suddenly saw two Russian fighter jets flying next to us. They were so close we could see the pilots in their cockpits."

As we flew over the Finland Lake District we suddenly saw two Russian fighter jets flying next to us. They were so close we could see the pilots in their cockpits. They stayed alongside us for awhile and then flew off. I still do not understand the reason or possible justification for their close proximity because we were not in Soviet air space.

Typically we flew with a crew of five: the captain, the co-pilot, the navigator, the mechanic, and one stewardess. Depending on the plane, we carried 28 or 32 passengers. We all looked to the captain for direction – he was the boss. He was also our father figure. We got to know each other very well and, as I have said, we really were an airborne family. Lufthansa actually began with TWA and Pan Am pilots from the United States. Our German pilots trained in Arizona with the American companies. Once the German pilots were trained, they returned to Germany to work with Lufthansa and Flugdienst, which became Condor.

Our German captains had flown with the Luftwaffe during the war, but they did not talk very much about it. Our chief pilot, Felix Müller, and his friend, Adolph Rudolphi, had served together during the war and after the war had worked as taxi drivers in Mannheim before coming to work with Lufthansa and Condor. Both were fabulous pilots and both became good friends. I still have a wonderful picture of Captain Müller and me in Munich eating chicken with our hands and drinking beer from a small barrel. I was never frightened flying with Captain Müller even though he was a bit of a dare devil as a result of his wartime flying. He also was a great storyteller. He once told me how he was shot down over Belgium and was parachuting to safety when he got stuck in a tree. It was night and he was terrified of what might happen if he were spotted in the tree in the morning. He decided that he had to cut himself loose even though it would result in falling to the ground and possible injury. However, he had to take the chance; so when the last piece of rope was cut from the parachute, down he went. He was only 6 inches from the ground!

Captain Müller was such a good storyteller. Another even more unbelievable war story involved him being shot down again over Munich and parachuting again out of his plane. This time he landed on the roof of a house and found his way inside through an open window. As it turned out, the people who lived on the top floor were away in their bunker, but before leaving they had prepared the room for a wedding reception to be held on their return. They had been saving for months, and the food and drinks were

A crew picnic outside Helsinki

all laid out in preparation for their guests. As one might guess, this hungry German aviator, happy to be alive, helped himself to dinner. He ate and drank his fill, then settled into an easy chair and went soundly to sleep. He was awakened when the very surprised family returned home after the bombing had stopped. Amazingly, no one was angry, so he thanked them all and made his way back to his unit.

Felix Müller was a very heavy black coffee drinker. Too much, I thought, and so on one flight I surprised him with a cup of bouillon instead of coffee. After drinking it he said, "This would be even better if you added an egg." Of course we had no eggs, but when we were in Tangier with an overnight stay he suggested, "Why don't you try to get some eggs?" So off I went to the market where some of the locals were sitting on the curb with their eggs in front of them on a cloth. I saw one woman who picked up an egg and put it to her ear, to see if there was a chick in there I suppose. I did not want to buy eggs from her so I asked a policeman where I could get fresh eggs and he directed me to a grocery owned by Swiss people. On my way back to the Rif Hotel I passed Captain Müller's room. The door was open and because he was our Chief Pilot and I was the Chief Stewardess, he asked me to come in and talk about future flights. When the rest of the crew arrived I left, forgetting the eggs. The next morning we all were waiting in the lobby, and Captain Müller was late. He was never late but, as it turns out, this morning there was a reason for him to be late. When he had poked one of the eggs with a pin to drink it, he ended up with raw egg all over his uniform. He had attempted to wash it off, but that had made a bigger mess. He was quite a sight!

> "I loved to fly with either of them. They were great gentlemen, and on the ground we always went out together as a family."

I made most of my flights with Captain Müller and his friend, Captain Rudolphi, both twice my age and like fathers to me. I loved to fly with either of them. They were great gentlemen, and on the ground we always went out together as a family. We soon knew who wanted his coffee black and who wanted milk, who wanted water and who wanted tea. During the war both Müller and Rudolphi served in the same Luftwaffe squadron, the "Fliegende Sau" or the "Flying Sow." As I have said, although both had been very successful fighter pilots, neither of them every talked much about their war experiences. Much later, when I lived in Chicago, many captains and crew members came to visit, and it was like "old home week."

Captain Erich Stocker was younger than Müller and Rudolphi. I made some flights to London and Brussels with him. I am sure that he was in love with me because he often said, "Fräulein Fasterding, you can still become Mrs. Stocker you know." But he was just not my type. Once, we were flying a Viking home without passengers after a flight to Brussels; we called that "ferrying." Usch Schröder and I were all alone and relaxed, so we put our feet up and were doing our nails when Captain Stocker turned on the light indicating that we should come to the cockpit. "Let him wait," Usch said, "we don't have any passengers." We took our time and waited at least 5 minutes before we finally went to the cockpit. Captain Stocker seemed annoyed that we had ignored his light and asked, "Didn't you see my signal?" Yes," we said, "but we were doing our nails." Now he was really annoyed! "Someone could have been sick and you should have come right away" he insisted. "Were you sick?" one of us asked." "No," he said, "but I wanted a cup of coffee." That was Captain Stocker.

I remember most of the other pilots. There was Captain von Tettenborn who flew us through a tremendous thunderstorm in the Rhone valley. He called me up into the cockpit and said, "Look ahead." It was totally black. He then said to me, "Well, we can't go over and we can't go under, we can't go around, so we have to go through. Go back and collect as many plates as you can, and we'll see just how good a stewardess you are." So I regained my composure and headed back into the cabin. Before I could collect any plates the plane dropped and I was thrown onto the floor. Bags and coats flew out of the open storage compartments above the seats and as I was getting up, I noticed one of the passengers, a lady with a very large bosom (as we would say in Germany, she had "a lot of wood in front of her house") picking potato salad out of her bra. When we landed in Lyon we asked the passengers to get off so that we could clean up the cabin. Two or three couples said they would not re-board the flight. I think von Tettenborn flew during the war; he was the same age as Müller and Rudolphi.

> "There is no faster thing than a Fasterding!"

Then there was Captain Mac Dougall, one of our British pilots born in Rhodesia. Mac Dougall was very tall and very gentlemanlike, and he stuttered. I remember once that he was asked about the altitude and the co-pilot had to answer because the captain could not say "seven." He was a great guy though. On one flight, when we were deadheading from Valencia to Palma Majorca, Captain Mac Dougall and I had to load the plane with sandbags for ballast. It took the two of us together just to lift them. Mac Dougall requested me to be his stewardess more than any of the other captains and when I asked him the reason he said, "There is no faster thing than a Fasterding!" How can I forget Captain McDougal? We all got along so well. I thought it was interesting that there was never any tension between the English and German pilots despite the war.

And then there was Erwin Zöllner whom I never liked. Usch Schröder was in love with him and although he never took her out, maybe because he was married, he would often come by with his dirty laundry for her to wash. She did everything for him and yet he kept to himself. I was pleased when she finally got rid of him.

The pilots trained the co-pilots, and I remember many of them too. Some were German, some British, and some American. There was Jochen von der Burg who had studied medicine but became a Luftwaffe pilot when he was 20. After the war he finished his medical studies in gynecology, but he was hooked on flying and came to work for Lufthansa and Condor. I flew a couple of times with him and remember that he always asked if there were good looking girls on board. He was what we called an "apron hunter." He would come into the cabin with his uniform cap and bend down to talk to the girls. He was always in the way when I wanted to serve. I suspect he had a woman in every town. Later on he became a 747 pilot and visited us when he came to Chicago.

The captains, co-pilots, navigators, mechanics, and of course the stewardesses all were part of the family, and every day turned out to be a new adventure. We worked hard and had a lot of fun, sometimes at the expense of our fellow crew members.

On one trip we were flying over North Africa when the pilot asked the stewardess, one Eva-Maria Wagner, to come to the cockpit. "Something important." he said. When she opened the door to the cockpit the pilot said, "Look down, there are elephants!" Eva looked where he was pointing but she did not see any elephants. "Here, look through this drift meter, you'll see them." "I don't see anything." "Well, press it hard against your eye, don't you see them?" "I don't see any elephants!" "Well, use the other eye and press hard." Eva still could not see any elephants. "Well we've passed them now" said the co-pilot, who had been listening to the conversation. "You had better go back to the cabin." When she returned to the cabin the passengers began to laugh and point at her face so she went directly to the galley and looked into a mirror. There, around

> "Look down, there are elephants!"

both of her eyes, were big black circles. She could not have seen any elephants because there were none, but the captain and the co-pilot had a good laugh at Eva's expense. No hard feelings; I am sure she recovered from her embarrassment before the landing.

On another flight one of our new and inexperienced stewardesses named Elke was called to the cockpit. "You're new, aren't you? Did they tell you about this wheel?" the captain asked, pointing to a small wheel in the cockpit. "No, no one told me about the wheel," said Elke. "Well, any time a passenger goes to the toilet you need to come up here and turn this wheel, it's what flushes the toilet." "Okay," she said and went back to the cabin. The plane took off and shortly after it gained altitude and leveled off, one of the passengers went to the toilet. As soon as the passenger had emerged, Elke made her way to the cockpit, opened the door, and turned the wheel. Very proud of herself, she returned to the cabin. Several times during the flight she interrupted her service to repeat the ritual of turning the wheel. When the plane landed to refuel, there was a crew change but Elke stayed on board for the continuing flight. This time she was prepared. After the first passenger used the toilet, she went to the cockpit and turned the wheel. She repeated the drill when the second passenger exited the toilet, but this time the co-pilot grabbed her arm and said, "What do you think you're doing?" "I'm flushing the toilet just like the other captain told me to." Well, the crew got a big laugh and Elke had a very red face.

> "They had put the plane on autopilot and had hung a sign reading, 'We can't hold it any longer, good-bye!'"

Once, when the cabin light went on, a stewardess went to the cockpit and was shocked to find no one there — no captain, no copilot, nobody. They had put the plane on autopilot and had hung a sign reading, "We can't hold it any longer, good-bye!" They were hiding in the coat closet. This was a ferry flight with no passengers and although it was all good fun, someone had to be the "goat."

We had no microphone in the cabin and so made all our announcements "live." We welcomed the passengers and informed them about the safety features of the airplane much as flight attendants do today. Then we handed out the "flight bulletin" that the captain had completed for the trip. The bulletin listed all of those things that you find on the television sets in our airplanes today, but they were filled out by hand and we passed them back so the passengers could read them. Most of the time they contained accurate information but on occasion, the captain would take a little "license." Instead of the correct destination he might write "sin city," and instead of the outside temperature he might say, "very warm," and so on.

Finally, of all the "notable" people I served during those years with Condor, I must describe three very special passengers on St. Nicholas day, December 6, 1957. Ludwig Erhardt, the German Economics Minister during the Adenauer years, was revered as the man responsible for the "German Economic Miracle" that brought normalcy to the German economy and saved us all after the war. Dr. Erhardt had chartered one of our Convairs to fly with his wife and daughter from Cologne to Nuremberg. Ulrika von Fersen and I were honored to be chosen as the assigned stewardesses. Because it was St. Nicholas day, we decorated the Erhardt's table with greens and allowed him to smoke his cigar. It was a special trip; Ulrika and I felt very privileged.

My oldest passenger was 92 years old.

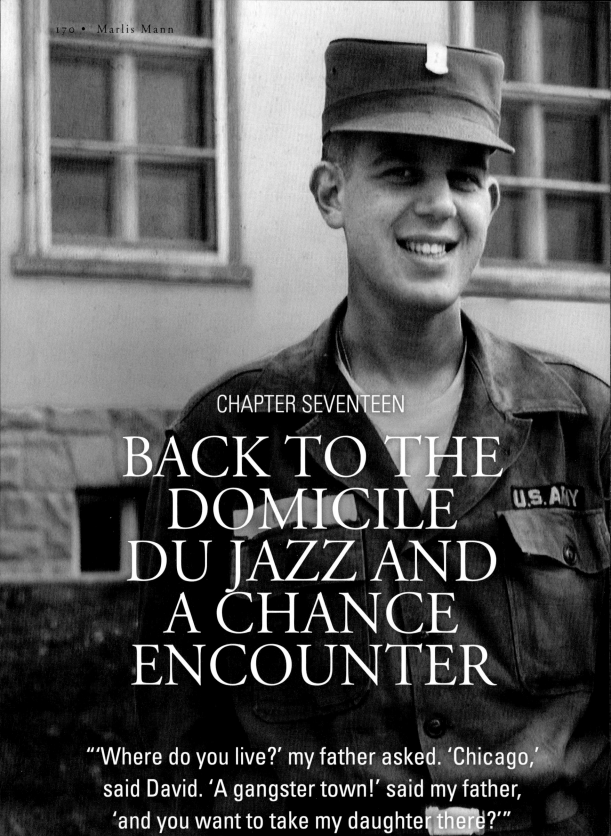

CHAPTER SEVENTEEN

BACK TO THE DOMICILE DU JAZZ AND A CHANCE ENCOUNTER

"'Where do you live?' my father asked. 'Chicago,' said David. 'A gangster town!' said my father, 'and you want to take my daughter there?'"

In those days the Frankfurt Airport consisted of just this one building

FRANKFURT WAS HOME THROUGHOUT MY FLYING YEARS, AND INGE WAS BASED IN HAMBURG. Braunschweig was only a couple of hours away by train for either of us, and whenever we were not flying and there were special events at the restaurant, we would go home to help my parents. In Frankfurt I shared a small apartment with my good friend and co-stewardess Usch Schröder. Usch and I spent lots of good times together out on the town between flights.

Although the war had been over for 12 years, there were still visible reminders of the destruction all over Frankfurt. The famous Domicile du Jazz club that Inge had introduced me to was located in the cellar of a bombed-out house that patrons accessed only by negotiating very steep steps down to the bar room, where they could hear wonderful, real jazz. The club was the gathering place for young Germans and visitors from all over Europe, and the musicians were the best. I used to love going there after a flight when we were physically dead tired but mentally still on a roll. Usch, Hannelore

Domicile du Jazz

Griesel, and I made it to the Domicile at least once a month, and other stewardesses sometimes came along.

In the beginning we had to bring charcoal to put in the stove because there was no heat and the basement was cold. We would meet first in a nearby building called "The Jazz House," where we could listen to records and buy something to eat. Then we would go downstairs to the Domicile, where there was only a bar but the music was live and featured the most famous German, Austrian, and French jazz musicians who were the "regulars" along with American instrumentalists who were on tour with the big bands. We heard trombonist Albert Mangelsdorf and his brother Emil, who played a great saxophone, and the wonderful pianist Pepsi Auer. The Frenchman Marcel Rigot played bass; and the famous drummer from Frankfurt, Rudi Sehring, played often at the club. They all were so great! I still have a recording of them playing at the German Jazz Festival in Frankfurt on June 8, 1957. American Jazz had taken Europe by storm after the war, and we still could not get enough of it.

Meeting David Browning Mann in Frankfurt on October 6, 1957

Another great musician I met at the Domicile was an American named David Amram. He was stationed outside Stuttgart and would go AWOL to come to Frankfurt and play jazz on his French horn at the Domicile. David was an amazing French horn player who came often, so I got to know him. Years later walking along the street after arriving on a flight to Paris, I spotted a long-haired bearded American who looked familiar. I first passed him by but then realized I did know him. "David?" I questioned as I spun around, and indeed it was David Amram! During lunch he told me that after looking for a long time, he had finally landed a gig at a place called "Rose Rouge." I saw him again years later in New York, and know that he went on to compose scores for the motion pictures "Splendor in the Grass" and "The Manchurian Candidate" along with symphonies, two operas, and many other works. David and I still correspond; it is dizzying to keep up with him and his non-stop career that still takes him all over the world composing and conducting music.

From time to time American GIs in civilian clothes made their way to the Domicile. One night Usch and I were having a drink at the bar and smoking our Viceroy cigarettes when one of the Americans asked us, "Where are you from in the United States, and where did you get the Viceroys?" When we said we were German he was surprised. "Where did you get the Viceroys? I suppose they were tax free." We explained that we

"Where are you from in the United States, and where did you get the Viceroys?"

were stewardesses and could obtain the cigarettes because we sold them on our flights. The GI's name was Bob, and when he next asked us for our telephone numbers we told him we were not interested but maybe would see him there another night. About three months later Usch and I met four Americans on the staircase leading down to the club. I recall that they were in civilian clothes and rather well dressed, in coats and ties. Two of them had very nice cameras hanging around their necks. Bob was there along with a fellow named Julian Erde, a young man from Texas, and a David Mann. "Mann, like the German writer Thomas Mann," I thought. "I'll likely remember that name." They all were very friendly, and Bob asked if we would go with them to a restaurant called Waterkant across the River Main to translate the lyrics sung by a woman they said was a singer of very funny songs. They said they could make out some of the lyrics but not the punch lines so they did not understand the joke. Would we come along and translate for them? Usch and I debated but in the end decided that it would be good for German/American friendship and besides, we had never been to this place, it might be fun.

The restaurant was noisy and filled to the brim, a very lively place. The boys secured a nice long table and along came "Ingelore," the singer they had been telling us about. Her songs were very funny and it was no wonder they had not understood: everyone was laughing so loudly at the punch line that they could not make it out. So we translated, and the boys were able to laugh along with everyone else. Ingelore was not terribly good looking; as a matter of fact she wore pigtails and was rather homely. However, she had a great voice and was very funny. One of her tricks was to follow people to the bathroom singing, "I'm waiting, I'm waiting. Did you wash your hands?" We laughed and laughed; it was a fun night.

Usch and I almost forgot that we both had dates back at the Domicile. We told our new friends that we had to go back and they understood. We took a couple of taxis and I ended up riding next to David, who surprised me by asking if I would be interested in going to the Frankfurt Opera. I was shocked! An American interested in going to the opera, could this be true? "Of course," I said, and immediately began to look forward to it. David said he would buy eight tickets and if I would invite three of my girlfriends, he would invite the boys I had met earlier.

> "'Are they American tourists?' 'No, they aren't tourists.' 'They're not American GIs, are they?' 'Well, yes they are, but they are all very nice.' 'Forget it' they said, 'we're not going out with American soldiers and you shouldn't either.'"

For 3 days I tried to find the girls I had promised to invite. "Who are these young men?" they asked me. "Their names are David, Julian, Bob and Jack." "Well, are they English?" "No, they aren't English." "Are they American tourists?" "No, they aren't tourists." "They're not American GIs, are they?" "Well, yes they are, but they are all very nice." "Forget it" they said, "we're not going out with American soldiers and you shouldn't either." Even 12 years after the war, even after we had escaped the Russians and were saved by the American Marshall Plan, Germans did not want to see their daughters and sisters with American soldiers, even if they were out of uniform.

Well, I had promised I would go and I always kept my promises. So we met at the opera, my four new American friends and I, the only young woman. The opera was "Tannhäuser" by Richard Wagner, and we all loved it. Imagine, Americans who loved opera! Little did I know this was just the beginning of the greatest adventure in my life. It was October 10, 1957.

David spoke some German but wanted to learn more. "Will you teach me some German?" he asked. "Sure," I said and gave him my telephone number. In the days and weeks that followed, when I was off duty, we met at the Mövenpick restaurant and at other restaurants, and I helped David with his German. I did not know it but David had a car. It was a yellow Nash Healy that, unfortunately, spent much of its life in the repair shop. He arrived in it one day and we took the first of many rides and dates around Frankfurt. Before long, David and I were in love.

I had never seen David in uniform and would probably never have made it to this point if I had. As I have said, German girls simply did not date American soldiers. If they did, they risked being considered "bad girls." As a matter of fact, one day when I came off a flight, David and his friend Dowd were waiting for me in the airport, in uniform. I walked right past them, not saying a word and not even looking at them, and went directly to the crew bus and home. Why could I not even acknowledge them when they had come to the airport only to meet me? Why did I feel that way? The war had ended long ago and I loved David, but I just could not bring myself to be with him if he wore his uniform. Thinking back, I know that feeling was ridiculous.

> "The war had ended long ago and I loved David, but I just could not bring myself to be with him if he wore his uniform."

As the months went by David and I grew closer. Then he returned to the United States to be with his sister Judy and the family for the christening of his nephew, Chip Chapman. David had strong family ties, and I knew that this event was important for him. Little did I know that back in the States he had a girlfriend who would be picking him up at the airport. And little did he know that this girlfriend would announce that she had become engaged to someone else while he was gone. I guess David was relieved that he did not have to tell me about her. He did tell me, though; and after all these years Niki and I still correspond. Imagine that!

On his return, between my flights and his work with the army, we began talking more and more about our future together. It had become quite clear where our relationship was heading. David's yellow Nash Healy continued to spend a lot of time in the repair shop, and he really wanted a Mercedes. So he prepared to sell the Nash Healy and began to look for his dream car. He located a used gull wing Mercedes in Würzburg, in the wine country about an hour and a half from Frankfurt, and we drove out to see it. It was a beautiful car that belonged to an army officer who wanted to sell it. Unfortunately, David wanted a new car, not realizing that because it was such a classic, the gull wing in time would be worth a small fortune. We drove back to Frankfurt and to the Mercedes dealership and there, in the window, was David's dream car, a brand new shiny black Mercedes 190 SL convertible with a red leather interior. "There's my car!" he exclaimed. So he bought it, paying $1,000 less than the price of the gull wing. He was pleased and proud of his new car as, of course, was I.

It was in the spring of 1958 and we were walking in the Frankfurt Botanical Garden when David asked me to marry him. I was thrilled but said: "I can't say yes until you meet my parents." So the next day I called my mother to give her the news and to tell her I wanted to get engaged and would be bringing David home so she and my father could meet him. She was pleased. "What's his name?" she asked. "Mann," I said, like Thomas Mann the writer. "What's his first name?" "David," I said. "That's not a German name." "Yes, I know, he's an American. Mom, you have to meet him, you'll like him." All she could think about was that America was so far away; would she ever see me again? Yet she was thrilled that I was thinking about marriage. After all I was 23 and all wrapped up in my flying career. I had dated lots of boys but never seriously. She was torn.

It would be another month before David and I could get away for the 3-hour drive to Braunschweig. It was spring but still too cool to put the top down on the new Mercedes. Our first stop was Göttingen to meet a friend. Göttingen was normally a 2-hour drive from Frankfurt, but in the new car David made it in 1. Braunschweig was still another hour away. I was so nervous and really wanted to get this over with. I so hoped it would go well. What if it did not?

I should not have worried. My parents came out of the house to greet us. The restaurant was open but with very few customers; summer would bring many more. There were polite handshakes for David and hugs for me. They led us into the dining room where my Mother had prepared a beautiful table and would serve a delicious lunch. My father drew a beer and brought a schnapps for David, and they began what must have been a fascinating conversation because my father spoke only a few English words. I guess David's German saved the day. It did not take long for my mother to understand that she could not change my mind and to see the loving man that I saw in David. She relaxed. After lunch my father brought out a cigar and David smoked it.

> "It did not take long for my mother to understand that she could not change my mind and to see the loving man that I saw in David."

There were, of course, many questions: "Where do you live?" my father asked. "Chicago," said David. "A gangster town!" said my father, "and you want to take my daughter there?" "It's really a very nice place," David told them. He would take good care of me in the "gangster town." He told them about his father and sister who both lived in Chicago and that his mother had died when he was 19 and away at Cornell University.

As we were preparing to leave my dad embraced David but my mother was still thinking "so far away!" I had a wonderful warm feeling as we drove off; clearly my dad and my mom had both liked David. This would all work out, even though Chicago was so far away!

Shortly before we arrived back in Frankfurt it grew dark and a beautiful moon appeared over the horizon. I asked casually if we would ever know what the moon is really like. It was the first of many dumb mistakes. I had cued David to tell me everything he knew about the moon. Back in my apartment he took my globe and a flashlight to demonstrate the relationship of the moon to the earth and I had to say "I am so pleased with the way everything turned out in Braunschweig. Let's save the lecture for another day." I would soon learn, of course, that David's interest in and knowledge of science was considerable. He seemed to know something about everything and if he did not, he would find out and report back. From then on I became very cautious in regard to my questions of "what and why?" If I did slip up and asked one of those questions, the lecture would come the next day. However, I learned so much; he was a walking encyclopedia. Sometimes it was a little intimidating, but I never had second thoughts. We were very much in love.

My parents at about the time of their first meeting with David in Braunschweig

With the successful trip to Braunschweig behind us, we could move our plans into high gear. David talked about an engagement party in Chicago where I could get "a peek in the box" and meet his family and friends. I spoke to my boss Eberhard von Brauchitsch about our plans and he was totally supportive. He arranged my schedule so I could work the flight to Chicago with David as a passenger and then we could stay over at least a week in the city that would soon become my home. It would be a 22- hour flight even in the Super Connie. I did the service during the trip and trained a new stewardess too. David got a special smile every time I passed his seat.

We touched down at Midway Airport and when I opened the door I could not believe it: it was like stepping into a sauna! I had been in many hot places from North Africa to the Middle East, but I had never experienced humidity. Wow! David left the plane with the other passengers, but I went ahead of him directly through the crew gate and immediately spotted my future father-in-law waiting with David's great aunt Elizabeth Browning. So typical of me, I never hesitated and walked right up and introduced myself: "I'm Marlis Fasterding!" We had a great conversation while we waited for David, although I know he was disappointed not to be the one to introduce me to his family.

"The week was indeed a 'peek inside the box,' a sneak preview of what my life would be like in Chicago."

As we drove from Midway into Chicago I was horrified. We passed through slum after slum, and I settled deeper and deeper into my seat. What am I going to do? I could never live here. Then we turned onto Michigan Avenue and everything changed. The city was alive and beautiful. We made a left turn that brought us to 72 East Walton Place where David's father made his home. I remember an old fashioned elevator with double iron doors and an Elizabeth Arden boutique on the main floor. The apartment was a beautiful duplex with rooms on the third and fourth floor. 72 East Walton Place would be our home during our 7 days in Chicago.

Long before our arrival David and his father had made arrangements for an elegant engagement party to be held in the apartment. They had invited 30 or 35 guests, some of them friends of David's father and a number of young people who were David's friends. I knew no one but spoke with everyone.

During the party a man across the room caught my attention. He obviously had a problem and for a moment I did not know whether I should say anything. However, I finally said to David, "That man's fly is open!" David was shocked. "Do you know what you just said?" "Yes, that man's fly is open." Well, in German a fly or a "Fliege" is a bow tie, and the man's bow tie had come loose and was hanging around his neck.

Of course, "his fly was open," I was right. However, I was gently corrected by my future husband and learned very quickly that a "bow tie" is not the same as a "fly"! The two words describe two totally different elements of a gentleman's apparel. I was so embarrassed.

We went on sightseeing trips, visited museums, and attended parties. One of the greatest occasions was a reception and dinner in Oakbrook given in our honor by David's very good friends the Whetmoores, who invited many very attractive young people. The American clam bake and lobster dinner was not only another first for me but also another shock because the lobsters were alive! I had never experienced anything like it. Our hosts opened the wooden boxes and out crawled live lobsters. In the midst of my amazement David said, "And wait until you hear them scream when they're put into the hot water." I was so gullible that I really thought they would scream, and David and his friends enjoyed the joke at my expense.

The week was indeed a "peek inside the box," a sneak preview of what my life would be like in Chicago. It even included a drive to Cincinnati, Ohio, to visit David's aunt and uncle, Kit and Graham Marx. The river in Cincinnati reminded me a little of the Rhine back in Germany. Back in Chicago there were more parties and more of David's friends to meet. Our engagement was published in the Chicago Tribune, and we thought we were the toast of the town. At the end of 7 days we flew back to Frankfurt together. It was time to make wedding plans on the other side of the Atlantic.

Our engagement photo as published in the *Chicago Tribune*

CHAPTER EIGHTEEN

THE WEDDING AND MY DEPARTURE FROM GERMANY

"…and there in the window was David's dream car, a brand new shiny black Mercedes 190 SL convertible with a red leather interior."

Schloss Hotel Kronberg

AS IT TURNS OUT, WHEN INGE AND I WERE LITTLE GIRLS IN TRIER AND MY PARENTS HAD VERY LITTLE MONEY, THEY STILL SOMEHOW MANAGED TO PURCHASE AND MAINTAIN AN INSURANCE POLICY THAT WOULD BENEFIT EACH OF US WHEN WE WERE OLDER. Even in such hard and troubled times, my parents were optimistic about the future. In my case the insurance policy provided the money that enabled David and me to invest in our future. We bought china and glassware from Rosenthal and silverware from Georg Jensen. It was the best; I was determined we would begin life together with the best, and David agreed. We were fortunate in one respect; although I made the purchases, David could arrange for the army to ship everything to Chicago tax free.

So the planning began. My father agreed to pay for the wedding but "no orchestra," he said. "Your friends from the airline will stay up drinking and dancing all night and I can't afford it. No orchestra." Of course I wanted an orchestra but what could I say? I knew my father's mind was made up.

As the location for the wedding we debated between Braunschweig, where I grew up, and Frankfurt, where I worked and was living and we decided on Frankfurt. We had visited the Kronberg Castle Hotel (Schloss Hotel Kronberg) outside the city sometime earlier and thought it and the nearby church would be a wonderful place for our wedding. Originally designed and built by Victoria Empress Frederick, the daughter of British Queen Victoria and Consort Albert, it was filled with art from Italy and France and until recently had served as officers headquarters for the American Army. So one day we drove out to the hotel and met with the manager who said, "We have never had a wedding reception here." However, he then added, "But there could always be a first" and agreed that "yes," we could have our wedding at Castle Kronberg. We were thrilled; things were working out just as we had hoped. The date was set: December 16, 1958.

As I said earlier, we have two wedding ceremonies in Germany. The first is a civil ceremony, which for our marriage was held in the beautiful old town hall at the Römerberg, which houses the Rathaus or Frankfurt City Hall. The square dates to the 12th century and was completely destroyed by Allied bombers but rebuilt in 1945. The ceremony was held 1 day before the church wedding and the reception, at Kronberg on December 15. Our witnesses were my brother-in-law, Robert Huhn the handsome head purser for Lufthansa who had married Inge, and Eberhard von Brauchitsch, the CEO of Condor. You remember it was von Brauchitsch who had promoted me to Chief Stewardess and through me he and David had become good friends. Eberhard von Brauchitsch was an amazing man. He was 32 when he came to Condor from the shipping company Hapag Lloyd, and he impressed us all. He arranged to buy the larger

Herr and Frau Albert Fasterding

announce the marriage of their daughter

Marlis

to

Mr. David Browning Mann

on Tuesday, the sixteenth of December

Nineteen hundred and fifty-eight

Schloss Kronberg im Taunus

planes for the fleet and made Condor the success it was. He was aboard on Inge's opening flight to Chicago, and now he was a family friend.

David was discharged from the Army and returned to the States by ship with his brand new car and all of our wedding treasures. On his way back to Germany, he stopped in New York City to visit his friend Julian Erde and celebrate with a small bachelor party. They were in a taxi coming to or from the party, I do not remember which, when David said, "I just got a telegram from Marlis and it said, 'I can hardly wait for Thursday when you are flying back'." "But David," Julian said "today is Thursday!" In the meantime, I was already at the airport to meet my soon-to-be-husband, not knowing that David had sent me a telegram explaining his mistake and saying that he would not arrive until Friday. I had left for the airport before the telegram arrived.

David wanted to take his first Trans-Atlantic trip on a jet, so he flew to New York,

My green card picture

visited with his friend, and booked his trip on a Pan Am jet to Paris, which continued on an Air France prop plane to Frankfurt. I was patiently waiting at the small airport and could see all of the passengers coming off the flight but no David. The crew and the cleaning girls came off but still no David. "Where is he?" "Is he asleep?" I wondered. Of course he never did arrive and so I went back to the office to collect my mail where one of the clerks asked, "Where's David? Oh I get it, he went home with all the loot and you think he's coming back?" And then he laughed. I was shocked, having never thought of such a thing. When I arrived home I found the telegram explaining that David would be arriving the next day. Of course the next day I went back to the airport and there he was. I was so happy the clerk in the office was wrong!

Marrying an American was a bit complicated. In the midst of all the wedding planning I had to go to the American Embassy in Frankfurt to apply for the green card that would enable me to stay in the United States. It took an entire day with papers to sign and numerous interviews that included questions such as "Was I ever a communist? Was I ever a prostitute? What was my Grandmother's name and was my father a member of the party?" When it was all over I was told to return in 3 days and I would have my green card.

In the beginning of December we drove out to Castle Kronberg once again to talk with the minister of the church, Pastor Grabovsky. He said to us, "This is going to be very simple; all you have to say is "ja." As it turns out there was a wedding going on at the time and Pastor Grabovsky said we could watch from upstairs, which we did.

Neither of us knew anyone in the wedding except the minister, but that did not matter; I cried and cried. Their wedding was so beautiful and all I could think of was that after our wedding it would be "good-bye Germany forever."

Our civil ceremony went as planned and afterwards we all went to a restaurant called "Will Höhne's Pferdestall." Will Höhne was a famous singer and guitarist and the word "Pferdestall" means "horse stable." Will Höhne had set up his night club in an actual horse stable located on a huge estate outside Frankfurt, and it still looked like a horse stable; some of the walls were missing. Höhne would come around

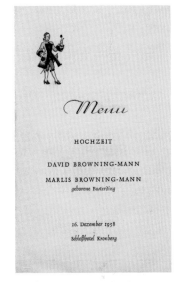

Menu

HOCHZEIT

DAVID BROWNING-MANN
MARLIS BROWNING-MANN
geborene Faarding

16. Dezember 1958
Schloßhotel Kronberg

Our wedding dinner

serving his famous drink, which was champagne in a silver bucket, to be passed from person to person around the table. You could not see the bottom of the bucket and so you never knew how much you were drinking. So here I was, the night before my wedding, "beschwipst!" I was very happy and more than a little "tipsy." As the evening came to a close Höhne gave everyone a copy of his record with his picture on the cover. I still remember the melody, and I still have the record.

My parents, Inge, Robert, David, and I drove to Castle Kronberg that evening and registered at the hotel. I was given the bridal suite and when I opened one of the doors of the armoir I discovered that two very famous people had once slept in the room. One was the empress Soraya, a young German woman who was married to the king of Persia, and whom he later divorced because she could not give him children. The other was King Farouk's wife, the "Begum." I called Inge to tell her of my discovery, and she came down to see the names and then put me to bed.

The next morning Inge came again and when I looked in the mirror I hardly recognized myself. My hair was a mess! My big sister put me back together, put on my veil, and said, "You have 5 minutes to collect yourself and come downstairs." In the years ahead Inge would tell and retell the story of what happened next. I had a tremendous hangover! I came down the stairs with the aid of the hand rail. Everyone was waiting in the foyer looking up at me and Inge said later, "I thought you were going to fall down." The hotel had prepared a tray of champagne, which I declined.

Eberhard von Brauchitsch had sent his chauffer and his car decorated with flowers to drive Dave and me to the church. The others had gone ahead. As expected, many friends from my flight crews had come to be part of the

friends from my flight crews had come to be part of the celebration. I remember that moment when we were finally standing in front of the minister preparing to say our vows and because it was very quiet, I heard my father crying. I had no idea he was so sentimental.

When the service was over we walked back down the aisle and out of the church. We were welcomed by a dozen or so uniformed pilots, co-pilots, and stewardesses who presented us with a model airplane that I still treasure. Everyone then gathered in the castle for the reception. We all were milling around when our chief engineer finally said, "Well, where's the music?" After explaining that my father did not want an orchestra, my friend sat down at the piano and began to play. "You have to have your wedding dance!" he said. So we asked that the carpet be rolled back in the beautiful "Green Room" and we danced to his music — first Dave and I and then the others. Then I took over at the piano with "In the Mood" and other melodies. Everyone had a wonderful time, even without an orchestra.

Around 5:30 or 6:00 the family and Usch Schröder, Eberhard von Brauchitsch, Robert, Inge, Robert's father and my parents went into another room with us and sat down to a beautiful dinner. I later learned from my colleagues that because all of my flight crews could not come to the wedding, they celebrated on their own for another 2 days.

The next day we drove off for a short honeymoon trip to Heidelberg and stayed in the oldest hotel in the city called "Zum Ritter," the Knight with the Spear. We had very little luggage and I was wearing the beautiful fur coat my parents had given me as a wedding present. We must have been quite a picture. The man at the desk asked for our names and looked at us as if to say, "Oh, I see! Here is an American GI and a nice German girl, here to spend an amorous night and be gone in the morning." Dave wanted to put our passports and wedding certificate on the desk, but the clerk gave us a knowing look and said, "It's not necessary." He then escorted us to the last room in the building, a tiny room with a tiny bed just large enough for two. The next morning after breakfast David asked to see the manager and after a brief conversation about our "welcome," we received a dramatically reduced rate for the room. You will not be surprised that I still have the bill.

We drove back to Frankfurt to begin the packing amidst several farewell parties culminating with a trip to Braunschweig for my last Christmas at home. We decided to fly and were between Frankfurt and Hanover when David realized he had left the

> "Oh, I see! Here is an American GI and a nice German girl, here to spend an amorous night and be gone in the morning."

Robert and Inge say "Auf Wiedersehn" at Frankfurt Airport.

large envelope containing all of our papers, our passports, our wedding license, and my green card on a chair in the airport restaurant in Frankfurt. We panicked! But flying and "customer service" were different in those days. A very nice stewardess understood our problem, went forward, and spoke to the pilot who telephoned the restaurant and connected with someone who could arrange for the envelope to be sent directly to my parents in Braunschweig. All was well.

We celebrated that final Christmas in Germany with my parents, Robert and Inge, and Robert's father, who gave me a beautiful dirndl dress. But the best present was the envelope that arrived, as promised, from the restaurant in Frankfurt.

On December 26 Robert and Inge drove us to the airport for our flight to Chicago. I said good-bye to them and to Marlis Fasterding. I was now Marlis Mann, and for the next 33 years, Chicago would be my home.

Frankfurt Airport, December 26, 1958

40 years later.

EPLIOGUE

MY NEW LIFE IN AMERICA

Marlis and David in Chicago, 1964

As I sit on the deck of the beautiful home that David and I designed and built overlooking Lake Michigan in Leland, and as I look out on one of the most spectacular views I have ever seen or will ever see, I am reminded of just what a lucky person I am.

What if our restaurant had not survived the bombing? What if the American soldiers had not come to Braunschweig? What if I had not heard "I Found My Thrill on Blueberry Hill" on their loud speaker? Had it not been for "Blueberry Hill," had it not been for the recordings of Louis Armstrong and Ella Fitzgerald, and had it not been for Club Marlis, I might never have fallen in love with jazz. Had Inge not become a stewardess for Pan Am, I would not have followed her into the air. I might never have moved to Frankfurt, discovered the Domicile du Jazz, or met David.

David and I were married for 46 years, and the Chicago suburbs of Wilmette and Riverwoods, Illinois, would be our home for 33. In Chicago he established his career at the R.R. Donnelley Company, where he became Head of Production Control. He also served as President of the Deerfield School Board and was Chairman of the Board of the McPherson State Bank of Howell, Michigan. I was privileged to serve on the Arts and Riverwoods Board and was Vice President of the Park Ridge School for Girls, a school for 13- to 18-year-old girls who were runaways from home. For 7 years I taught German in the Highland Park Adult Education program, worked briefly for Lufthansa in their downtown Chicago office, worked for the Encyclopædia Britannica, and became a travel agent. It was a rich life filled with wonderful friends, lots of parties, cultural events, and the joy of our golden retriever Charlie Brown. David and I were kindred spirits when it came to travel, and together we visited places far too numerous to mention.

> "David and I were kindred spirits when it came to travel, and together we visited places far too numerous to mention."

It was in Riverwoods that we raised our two children, Thomas Browning Mann II ("TB") and Katherine Inge Mann ("Kit"). We cheered for Tom on the high school football, swim, and track and field teams; and we were equally supportive of Kit when she played field hockey. Tom also played string bass while Kit studied ballet and played flute. Tom and Kit each studied in Germany during their high school years and, as a result, speak German fluently.

Tom studied at Dennison University, the University of Heidelberg in Germany, and American University, earning two law degrees before practicing law in Chicago. Since 1993 he has served as Managing Director of TransLegal Deutschland GmbH, based in Frankfurt, and now runs two companies from the United States specializing in legal translation and comparative law training. Kit graduated from William Woods College in Fulton, Missouri, with a Bachelor of Fine Arts degree with a specialization in black and white photography. After working briefly for Talbots, Kit followed her mother into the air as a flight attendant for American Airlines. Tom married Kara, and Kit married Bill; and both have beautiful families in Evanston, Illinois, and Cape Cod, Massachusetts, respectively. I treasure my children and my beautiful grandchildren, Lauren, Madison, and Emersen.

Late in his life David's father married Helene Palmer, who had summered in Leland, Michigan, for many years. It was natural for Dad and Helene to continue the tradition, and we soon joined them, beginning a rich social life in what was to be our summer home too. With David's retirement in 1988, life became even richer as we threw ourselves into the Leland community and built our dream home high on a hill overlooking the great lake. I continued my work as a travel consultant while David served on many community boards including as Trustee of the private Leelanau School and as President of the Traverse Symphony. He was Chairman of the Leland Township Planning Commission and a Share Care volunteer. We sang together in the choir at the Leland Methodist Church, and in 1990 I became a member and the Youth Exchange Officer of the Suttons Bay—Leelanau Rotary Club. In 1996 I was selected as the first woman President of the Club and it was then, after 38 years, that I decided to become an American citizen. I went on to become Vice President of the Share Care Board and a board member of the International Affairs Forum, the Glen Arbor Art Association, and the Traverse Symphony Orchestra.

It has been an amazing journey, from that first train ride to Trier to the view from my "Magic Mountain" in Leland today. I treasure each and every memory. Although these pages chronicle my adventures and accomplishments during little more than the first third of my life, I must say I am equally proud of my accomplishments in America. I am especially proud of my family.

> "In 2002, when David was diagnosed with cancer, we were introduced to an unwelcome awakening — the precious but finite quality of our beautiful life of good fortune together."

My journey has been amazing, beginning with that first train ride to Trier when I was 3 to the little bit of Germany we created by naming our Lake Michigan vista home "The Magic Mountain," to honor David's father, Thomas Mann. The Magic Mountain, you see, is a book by the famous German writer Thomas Mann, who in 1929 won the Nobel Prize in Literature for his book Buddenbrooks. The two men actually met when they both were at Princeton University in the 1920s, and David's father had received the "other" Thomas Mann's mail. David shared the familiar story with me, and we thought it was appropriate to name our beautiful home for both Thomas Manns as well as our son Tom. I have included a Thomas Mann quotation on the last page of this book.

In 2002, when David was diagnosed with cancer, we were introduced to an unwelcome awakening — the precious but finite quality of our beautiful life of good fortune together. Despite the measured optimism of the doctors' pronouncement, our almost limitless joie de vivre came to an abrupt end. As we resigned ourselves to learning a new medical vocabulary, we concentrated on fighting back as best we could.

Before his diagnosis, David and I had met Beth and Tom Skinner at a Leland party and had socialized together before Beth and David became fellow patients. Beth was especially knowledgeable and helpful in our encounter with this new reality as Beth and David were in the care of the same Traverse City oncologist. Beth practiced an "infectious" optimism of her own! She and I and David and Tom became friends, and I invited Beth to join me on the Share Care Board. We saw quite a bit of each other.

> "David's tragic passing, and Beth's, gave rise to my new appreciation for the relatively new friend whose life had suddenly connected with mine."

David's tragic passing, and Beth's, gave rise to my new appreciation for the relatively new friend whose life had suddenly connected with mine. Both of us went through hell. I learned more about Tom's career as a television program executive and that Tom and I were equally knowledgeable about and devoted to every art form, especially painting, classical music, and jazz. I thoroughly enjoyed his company, I introduced him to the opera, and we saw each other more and more.

Then in 2009 I embarked on yet another daring adventure to join with Tom in marriage. Together we now count five children and 10 grandchildren! I am especially proud of my extended family as we continue to enjoy "Act Two" of our rich lives together here in northern Michigan and wherever our travels take us.

Marlis Mann
Summer 2016

"What is success? It is an inner, an indescribable force, resourcefulness, power of vision; a consciousness that I am, by my mere existence, exerting pressure on the movement of life about me. It is my belief in the adaptability of life to my own ends. Fortune and success lie within ourselves."

From Mann Thomas. 1901. Buddenbrooks [Buddenbrooks: Verfall einer Familie, Roman]. Berlin : Deutsche Buch-Gemeinschaft.